# Beautiful Flowers Coloring Book for Adults

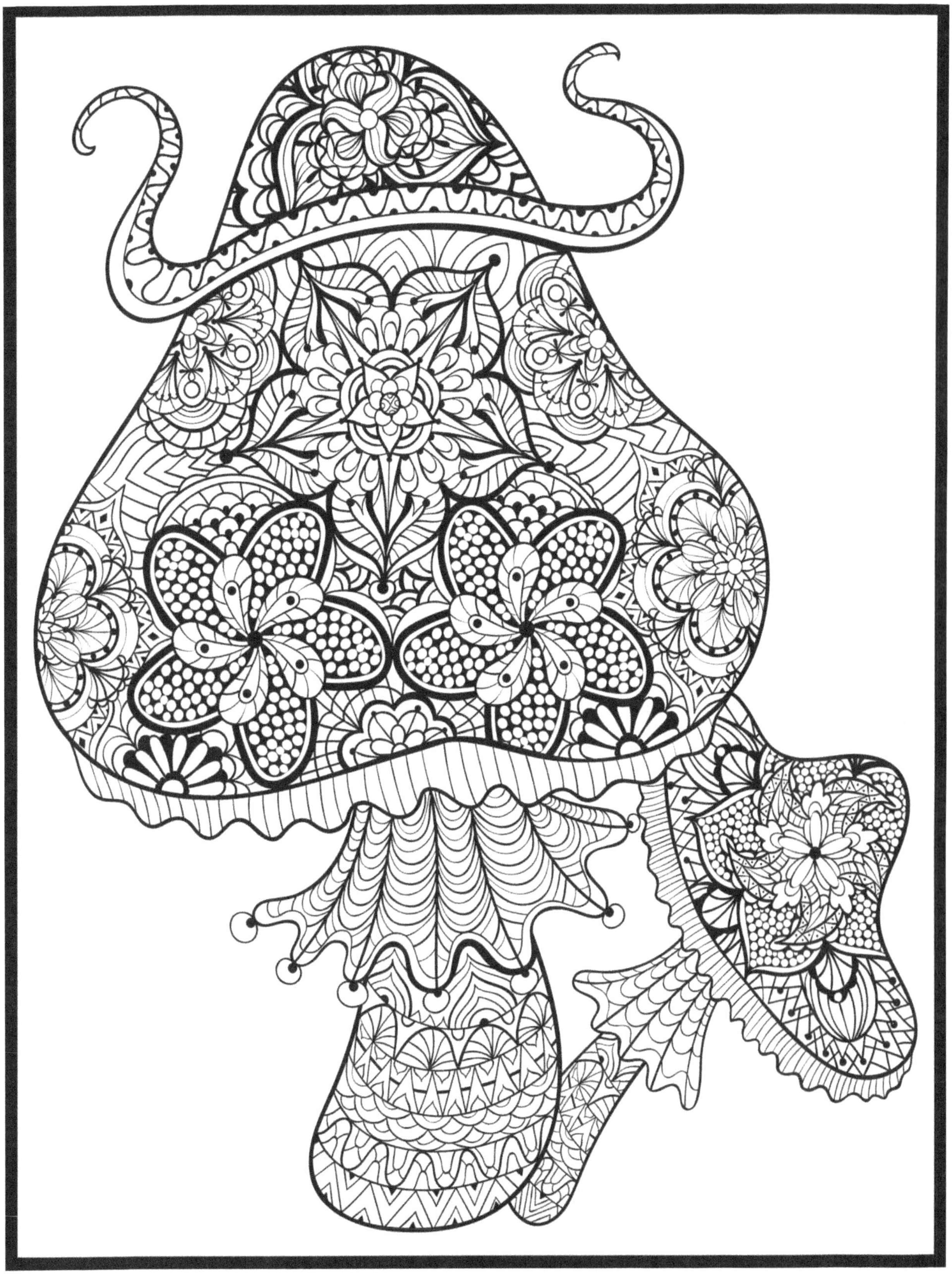

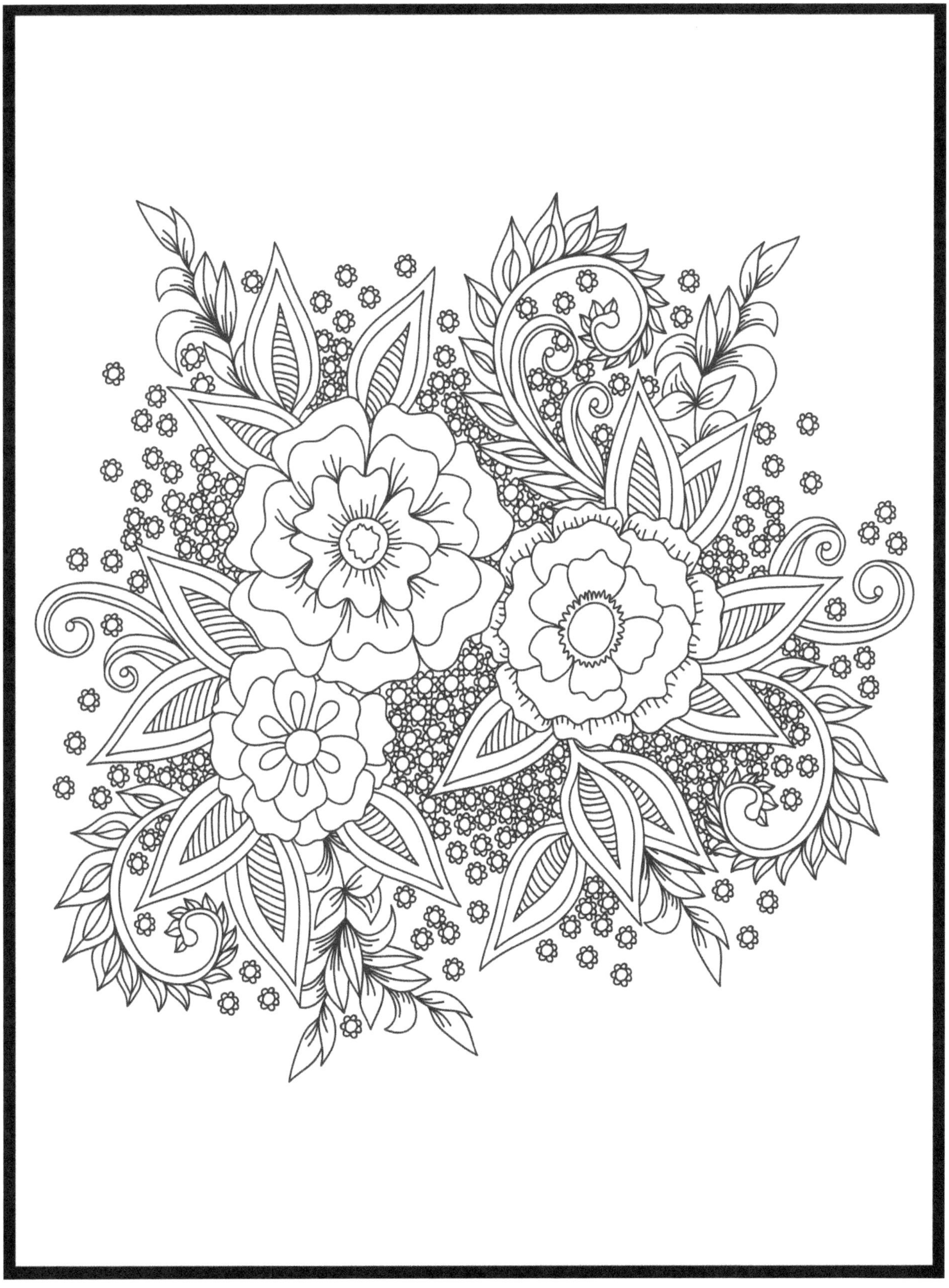

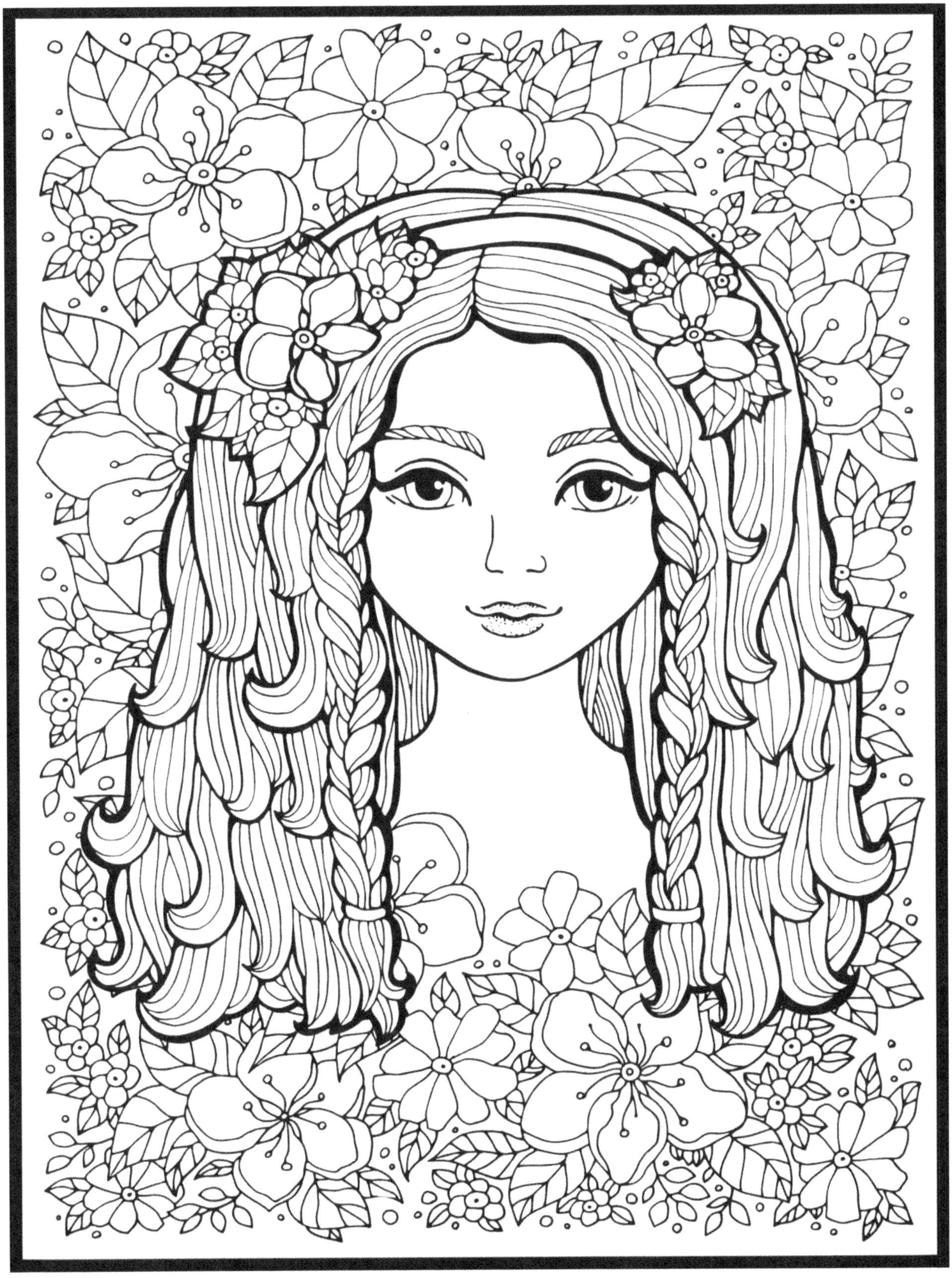

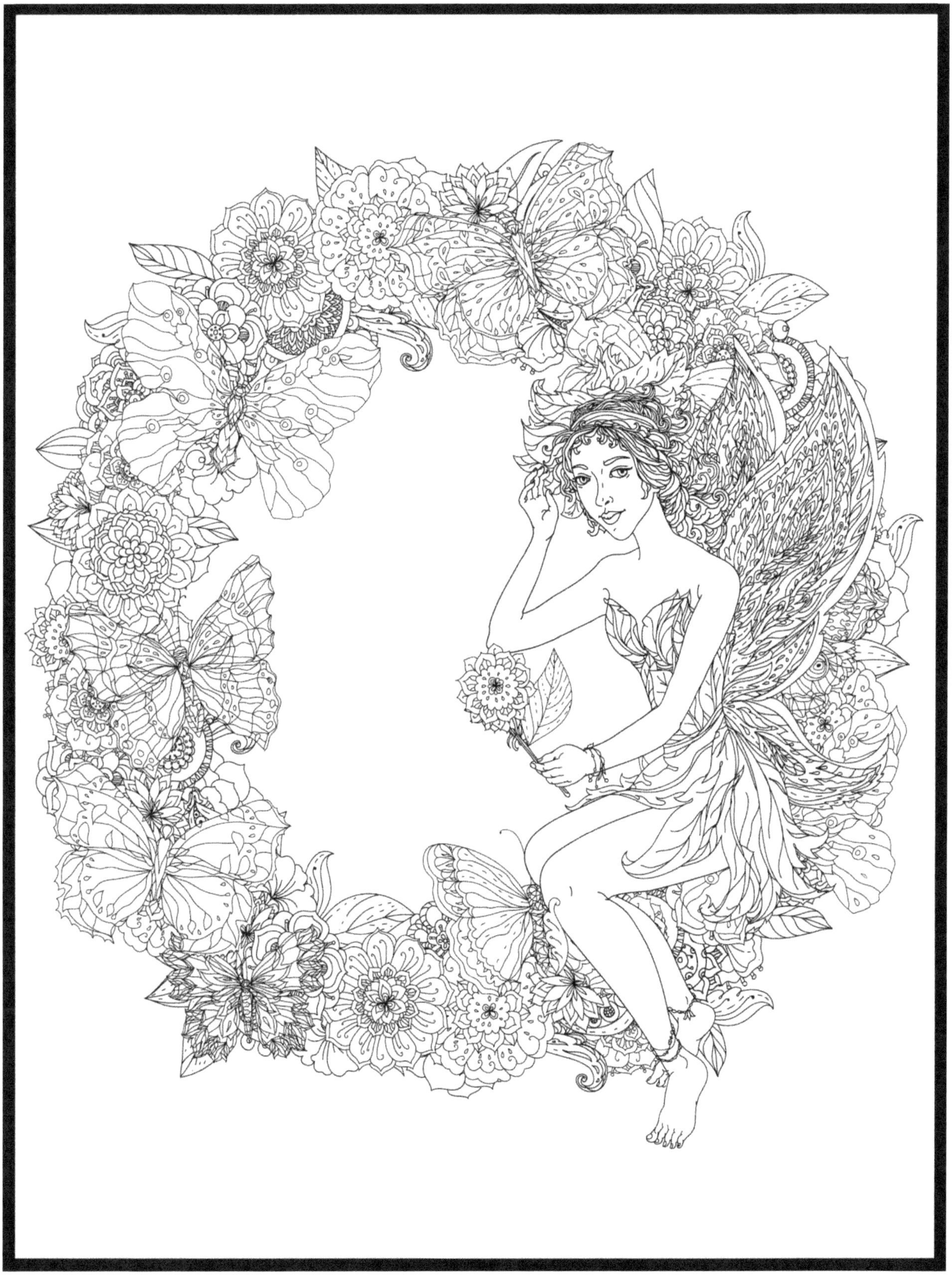

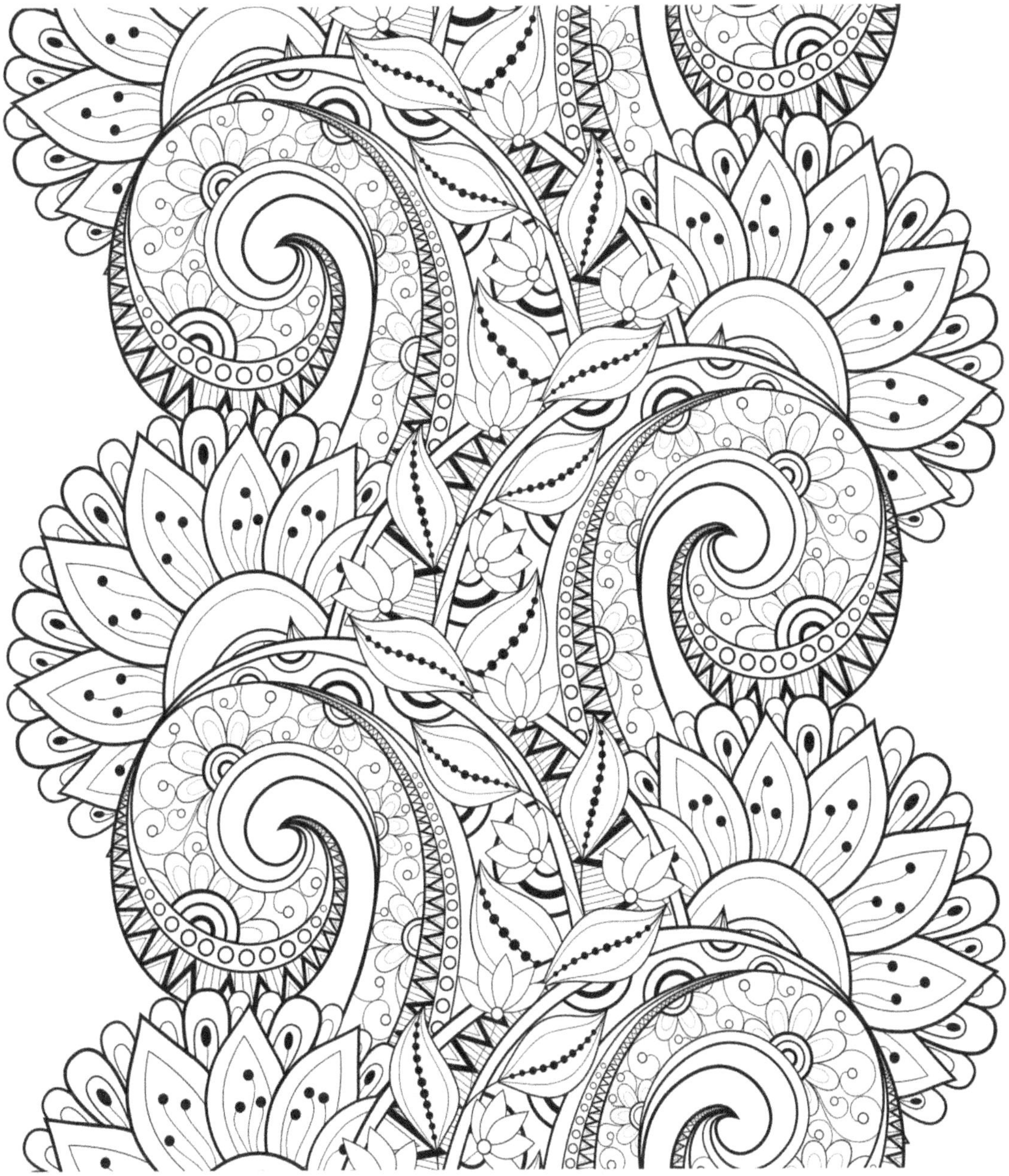

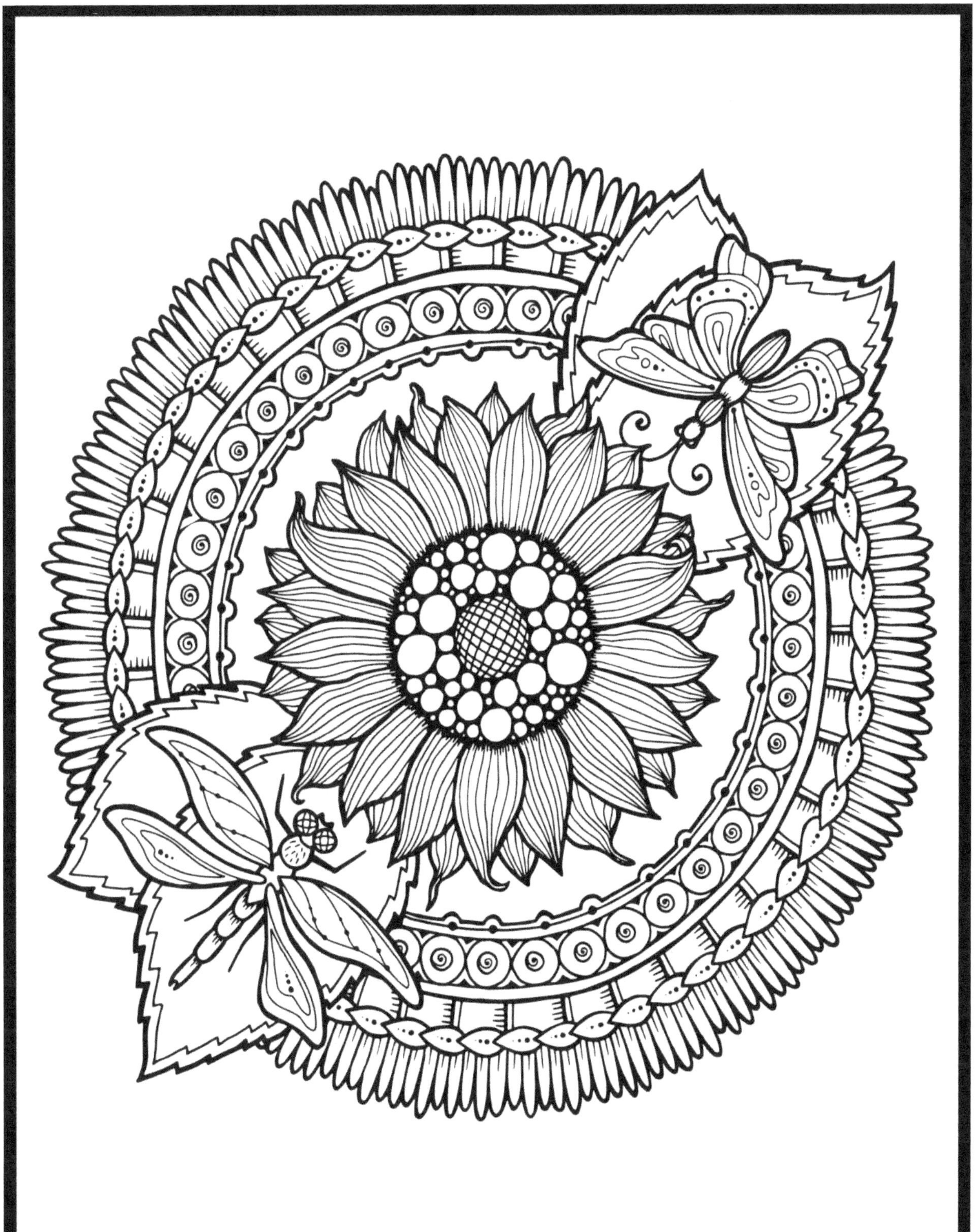

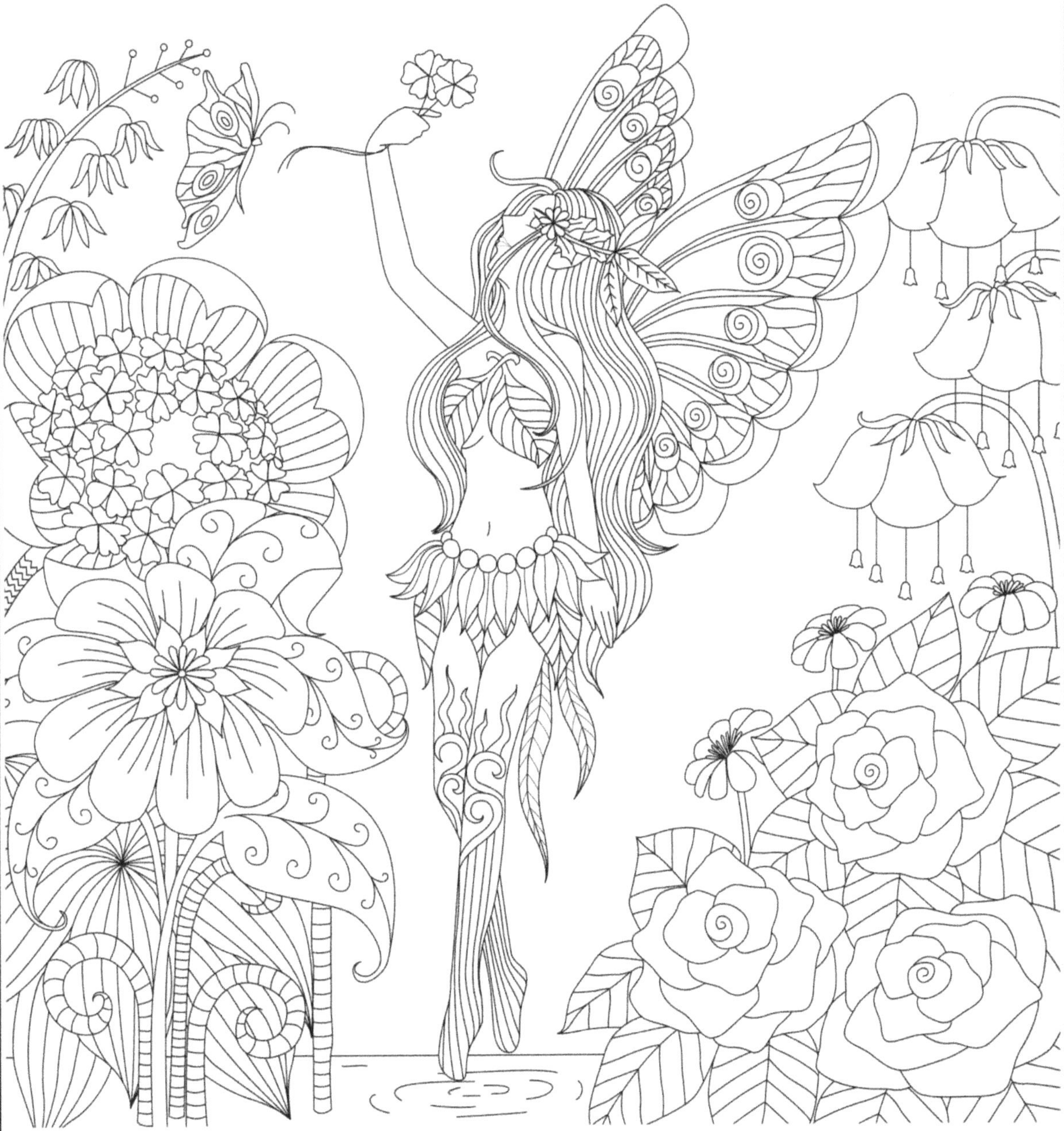

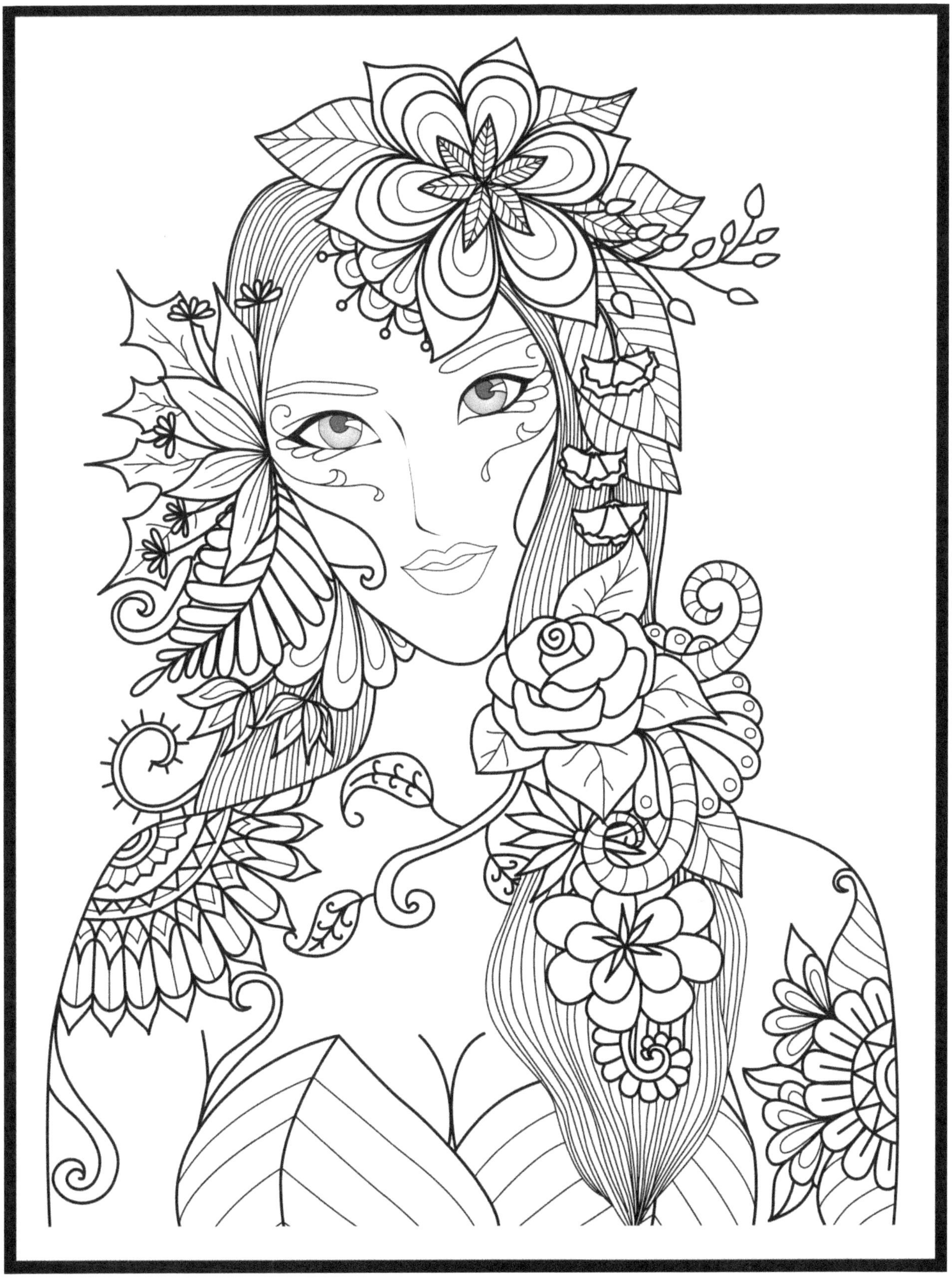

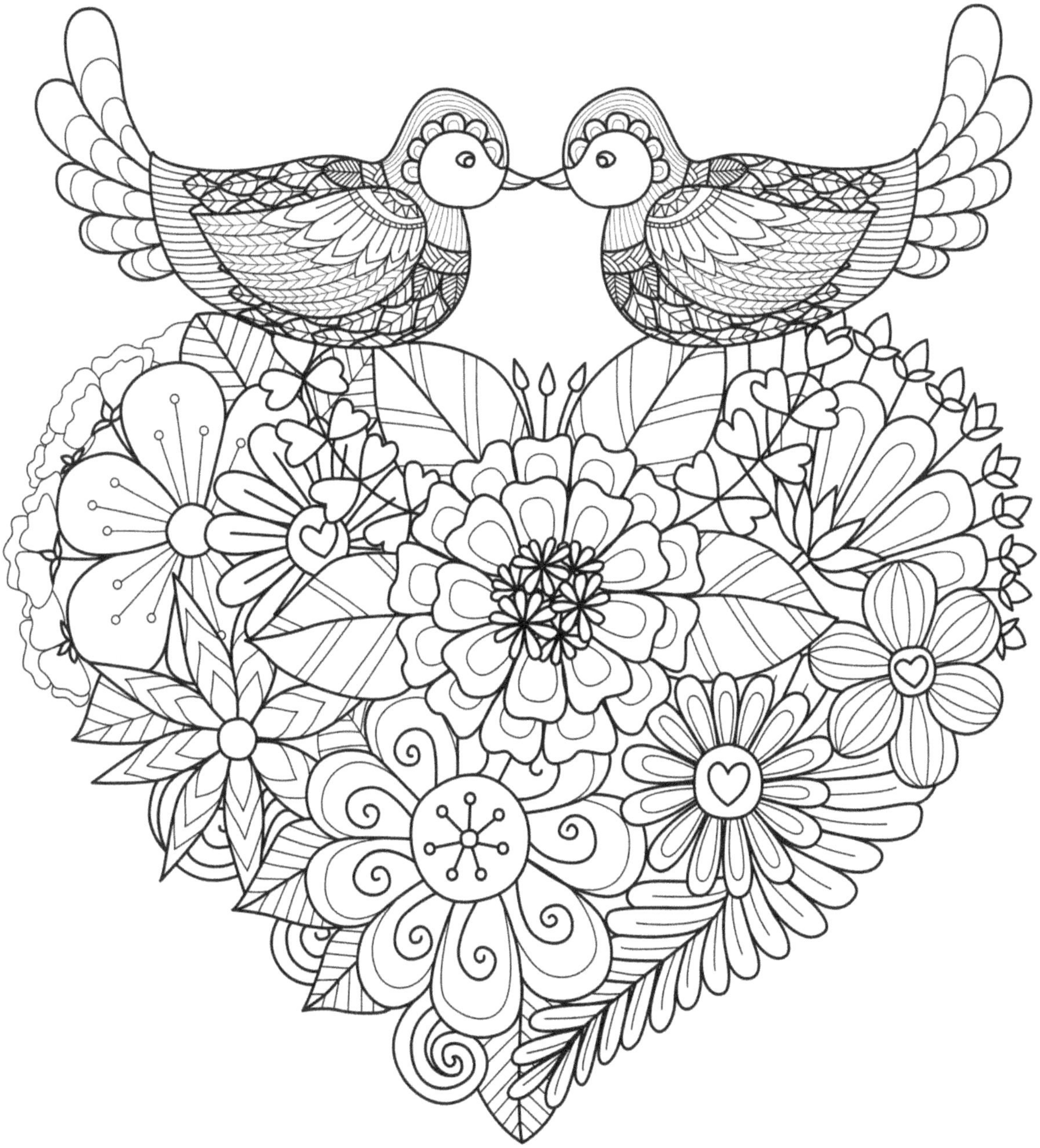

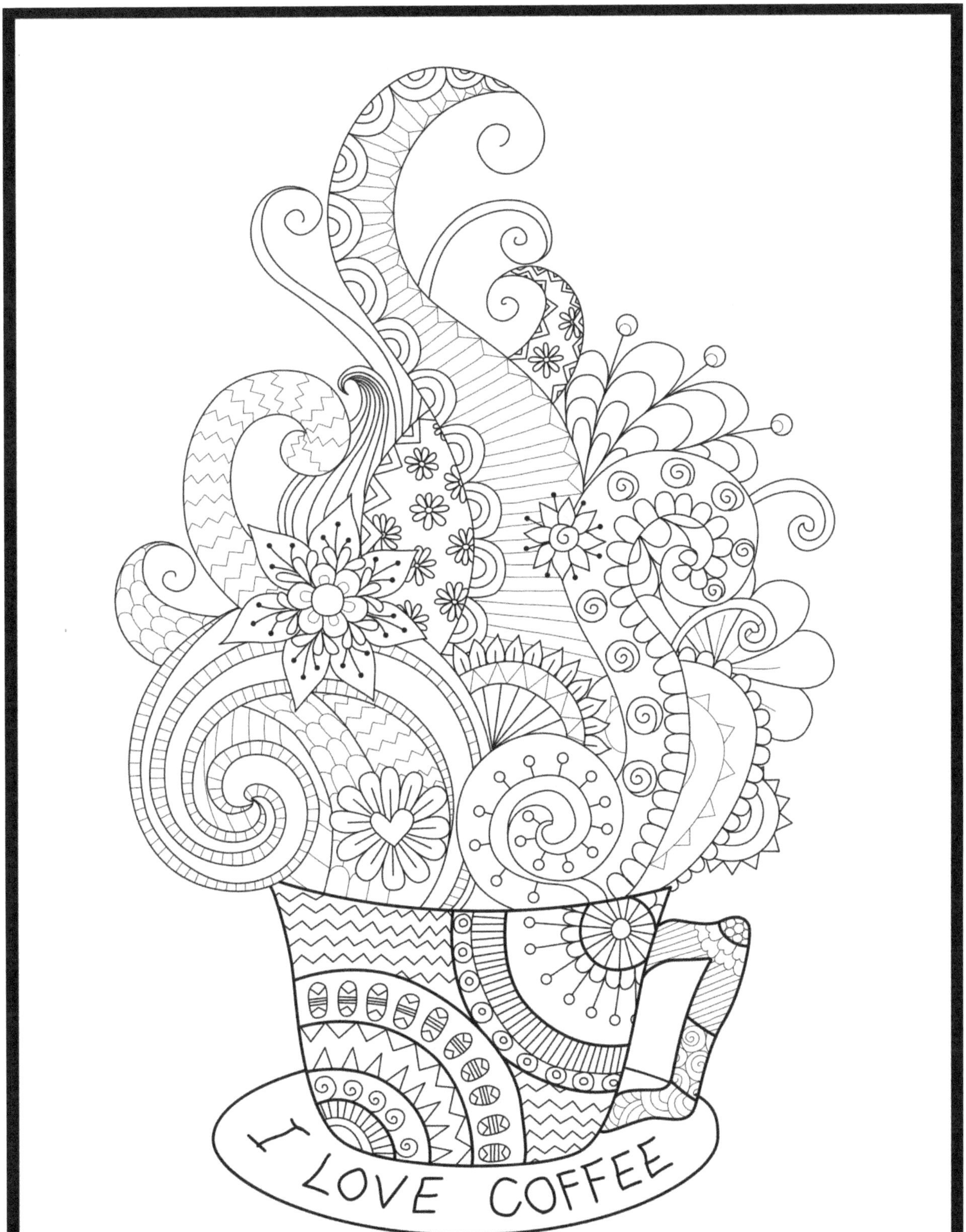
I LOVE COFFEE

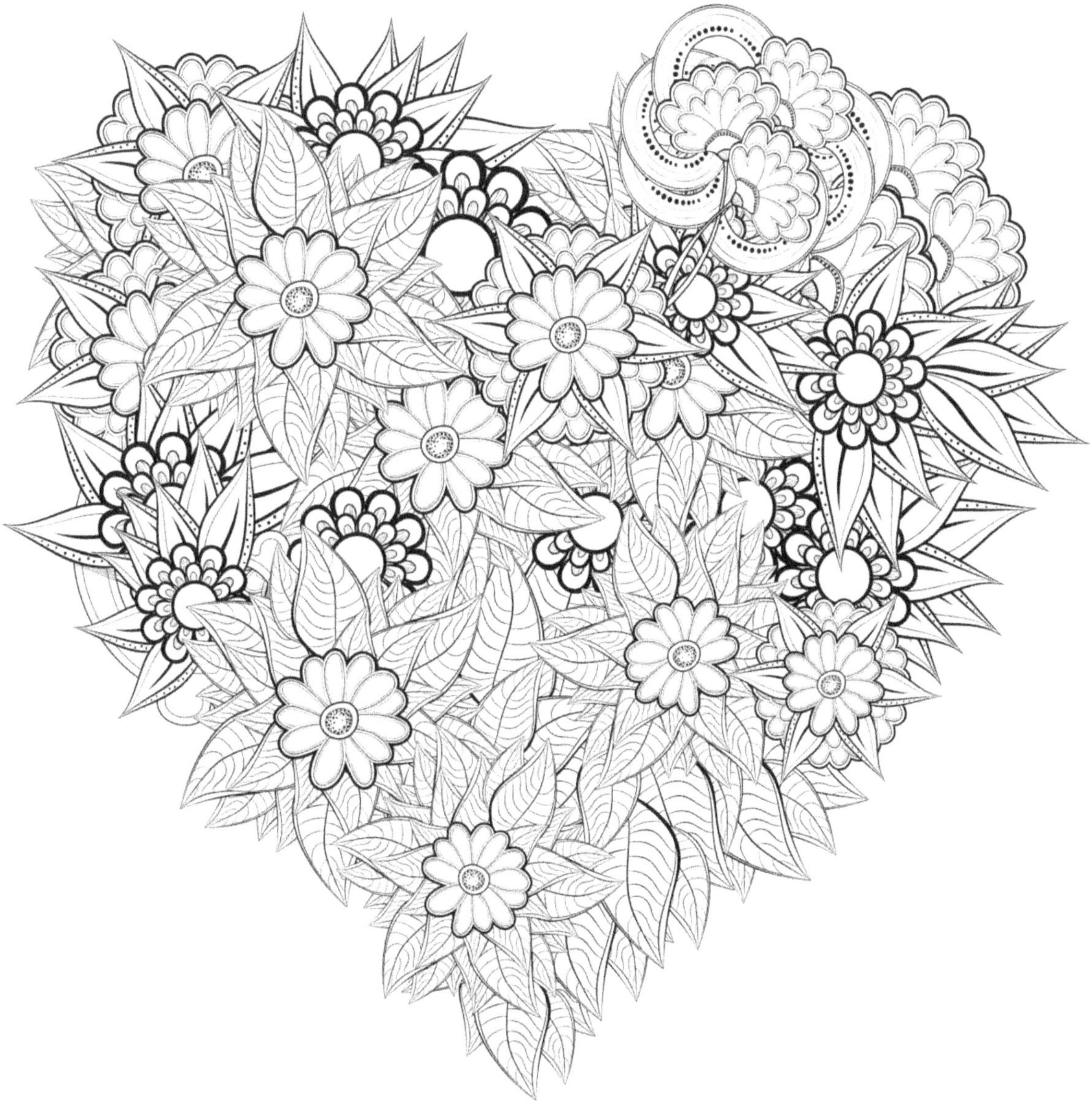

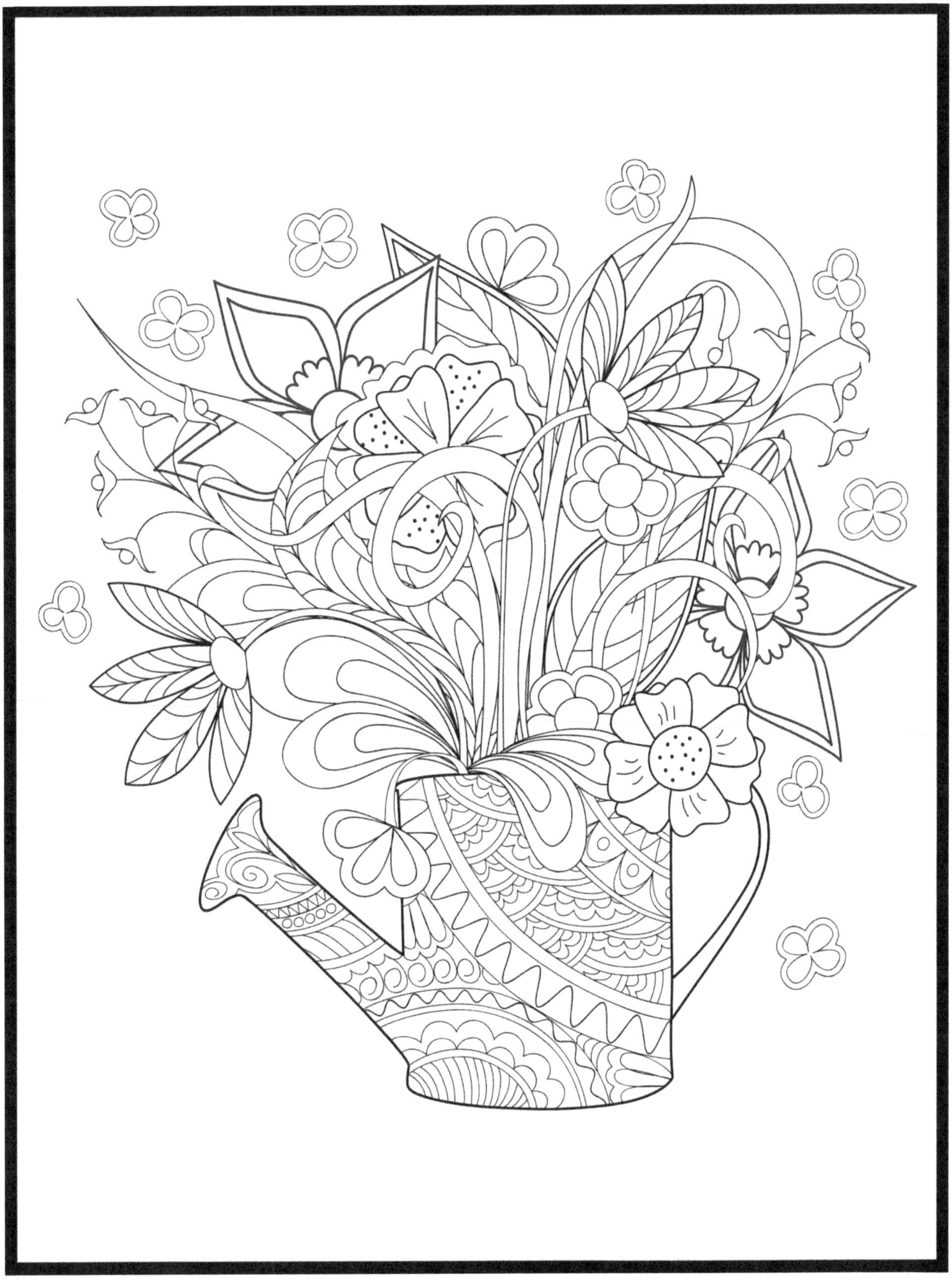

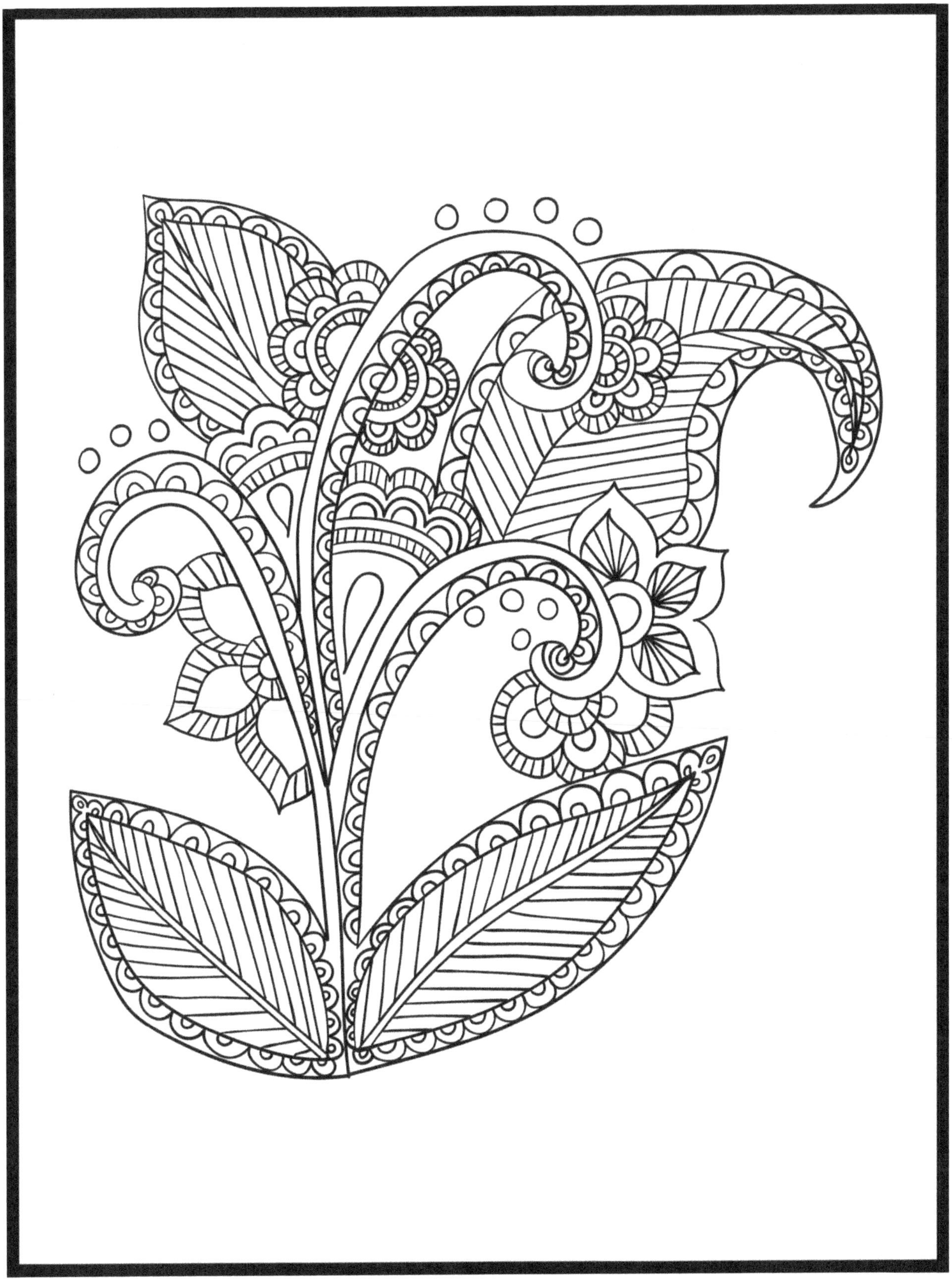

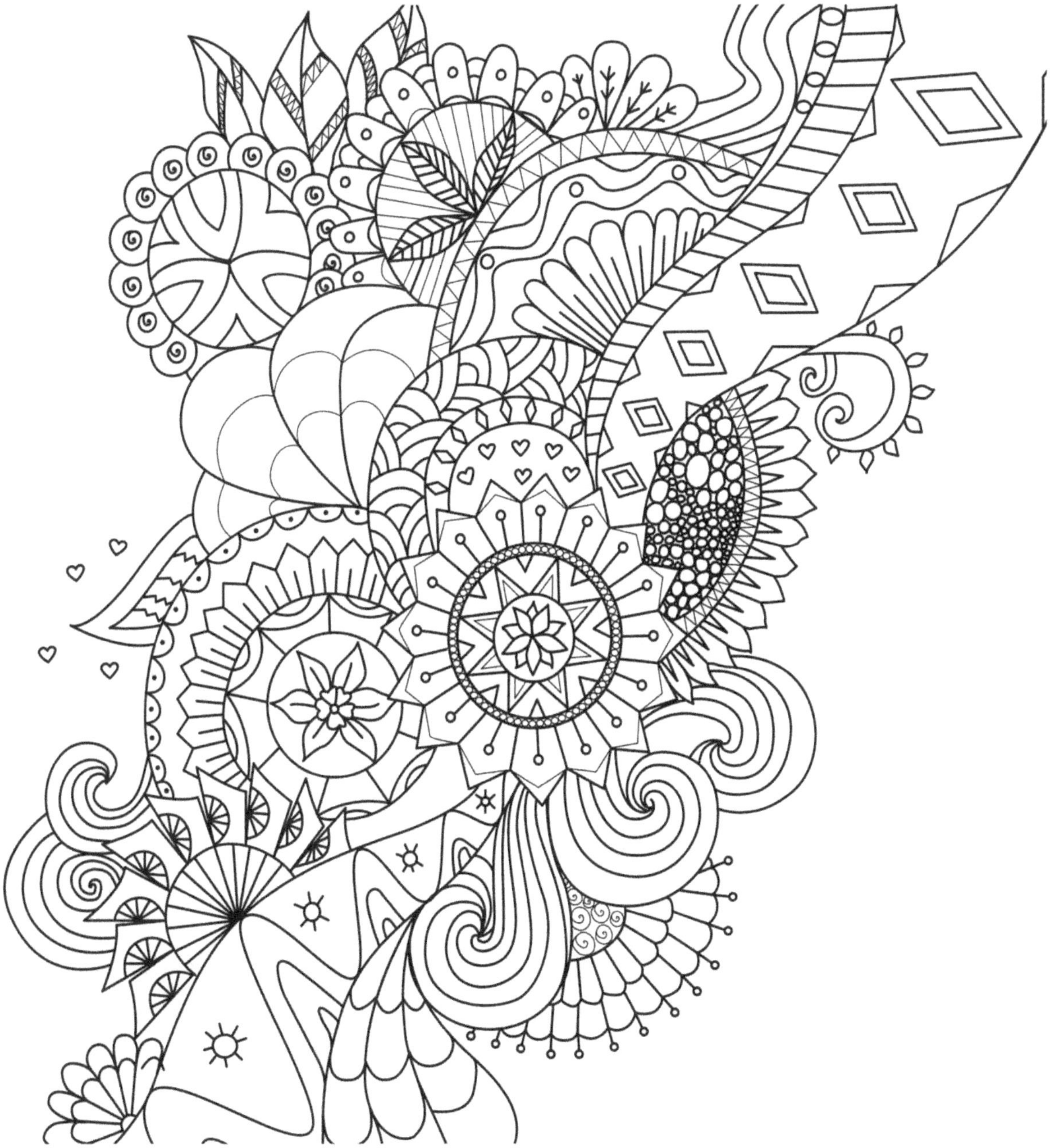

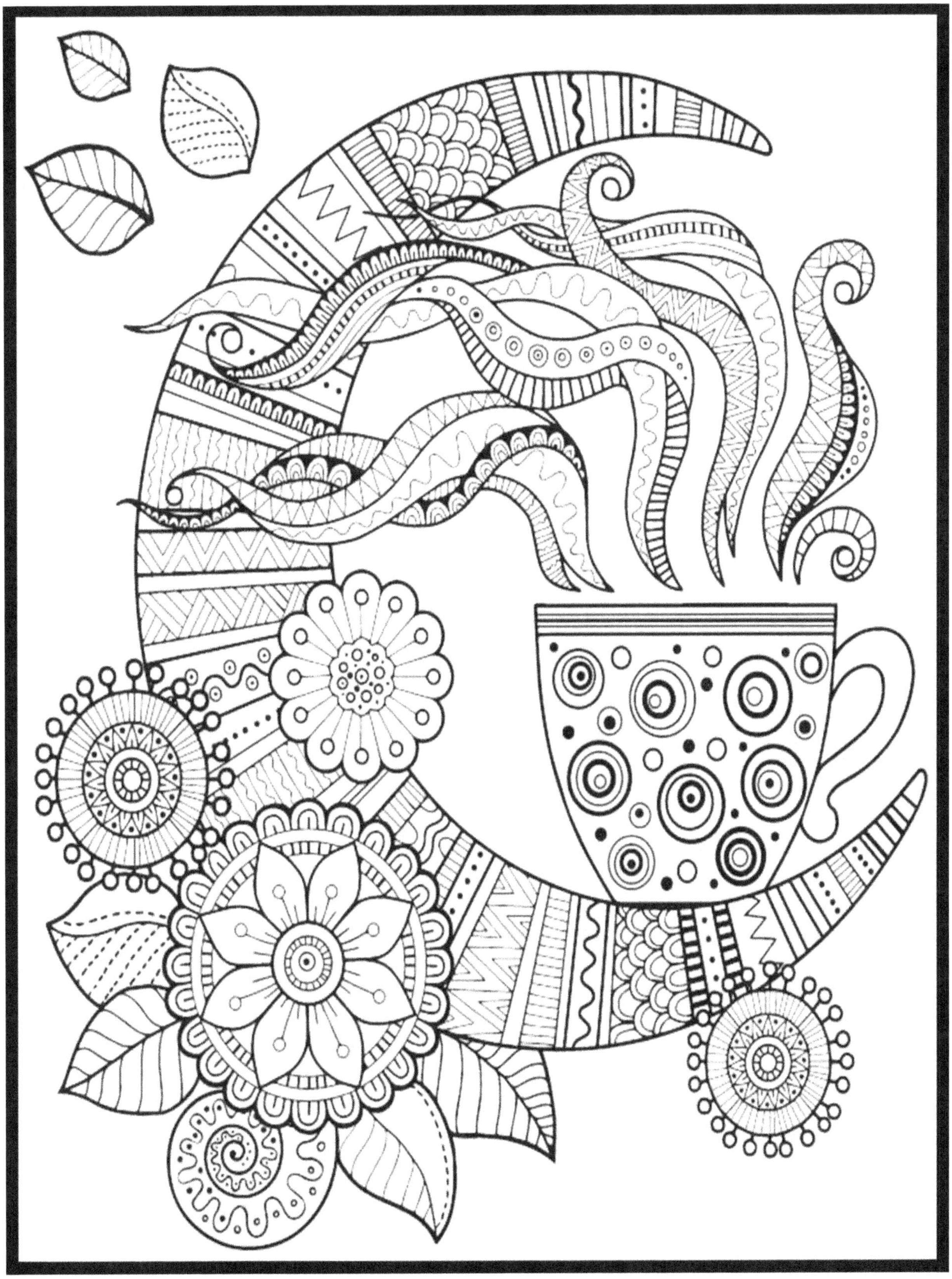

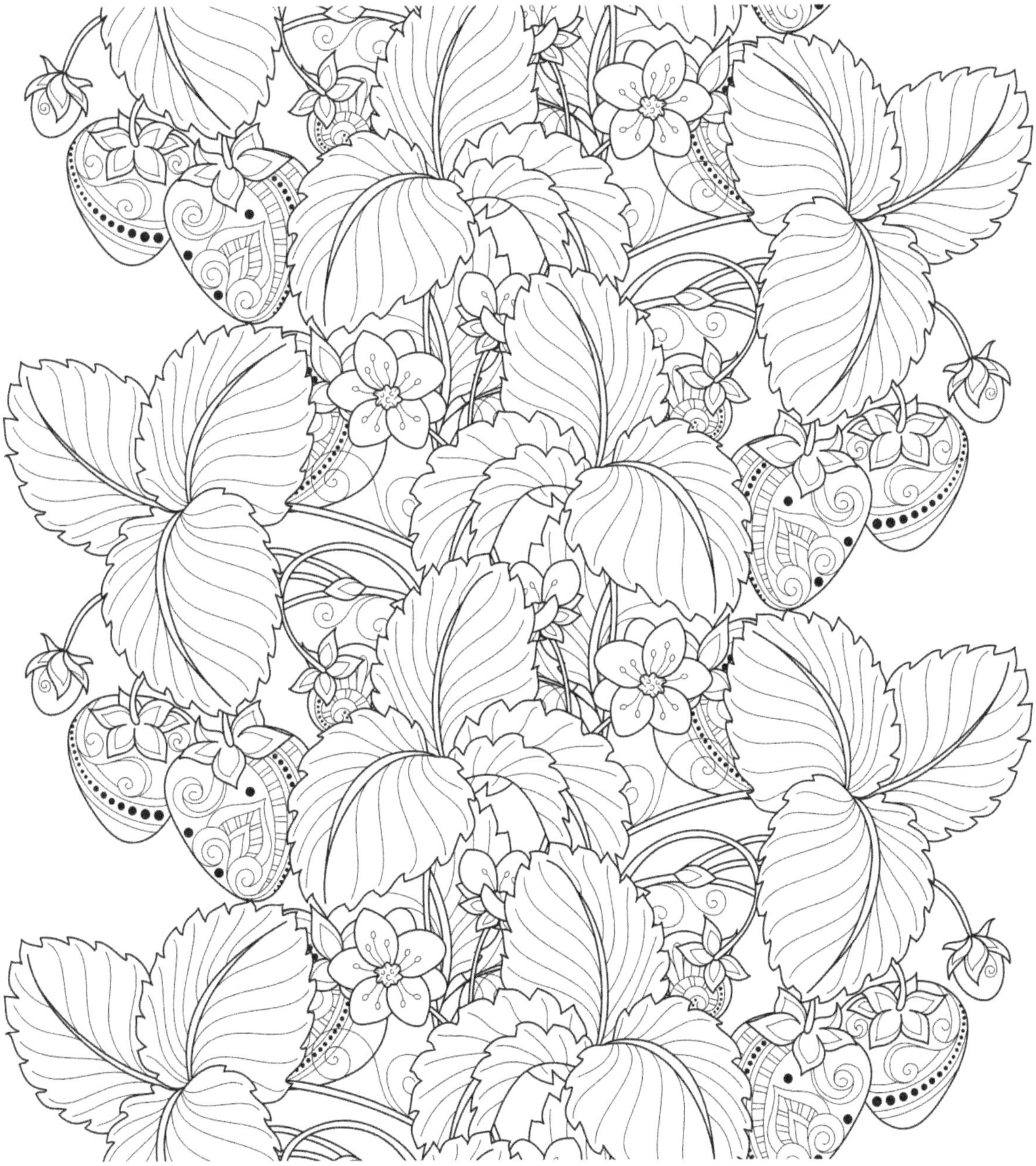

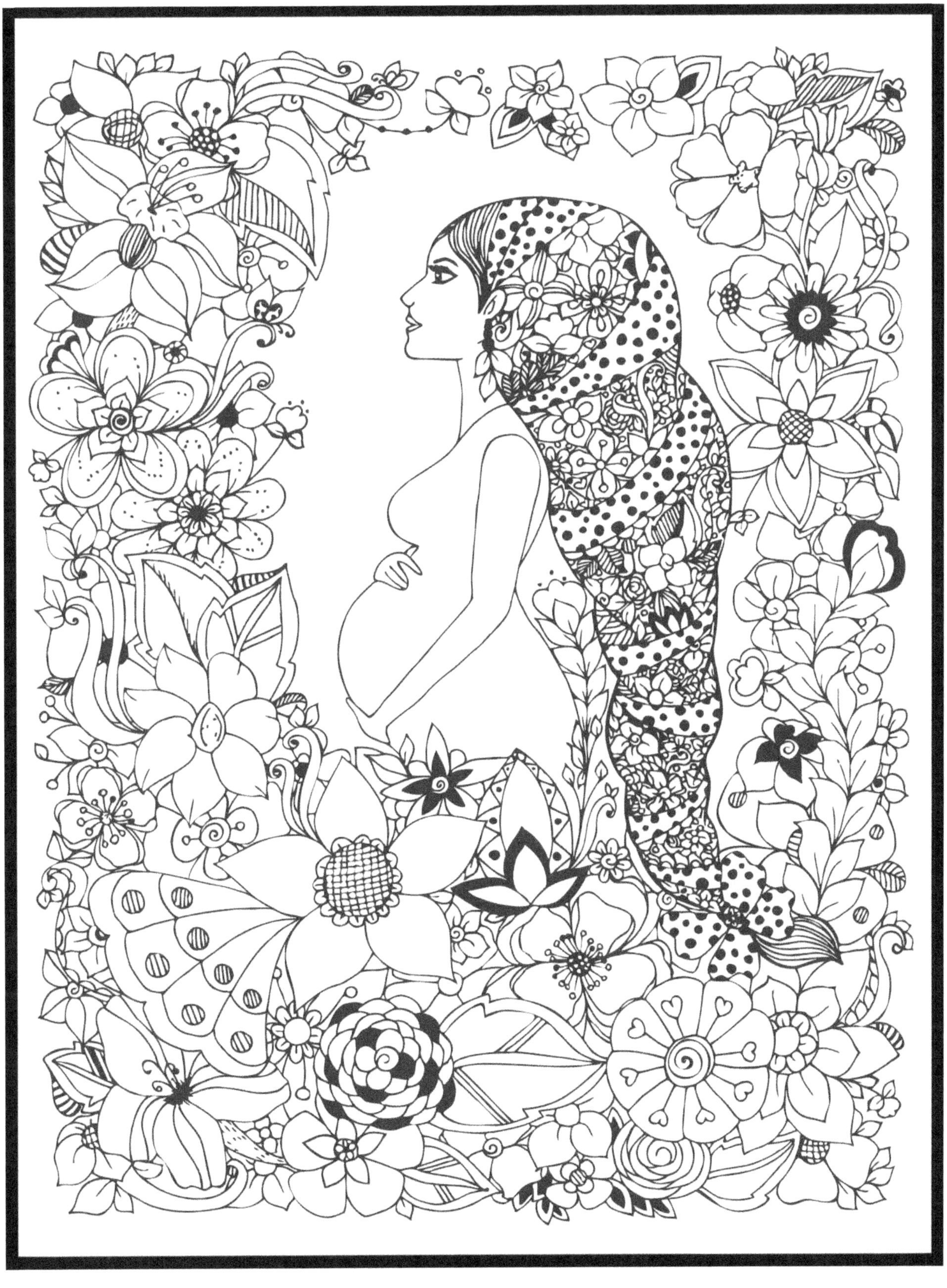

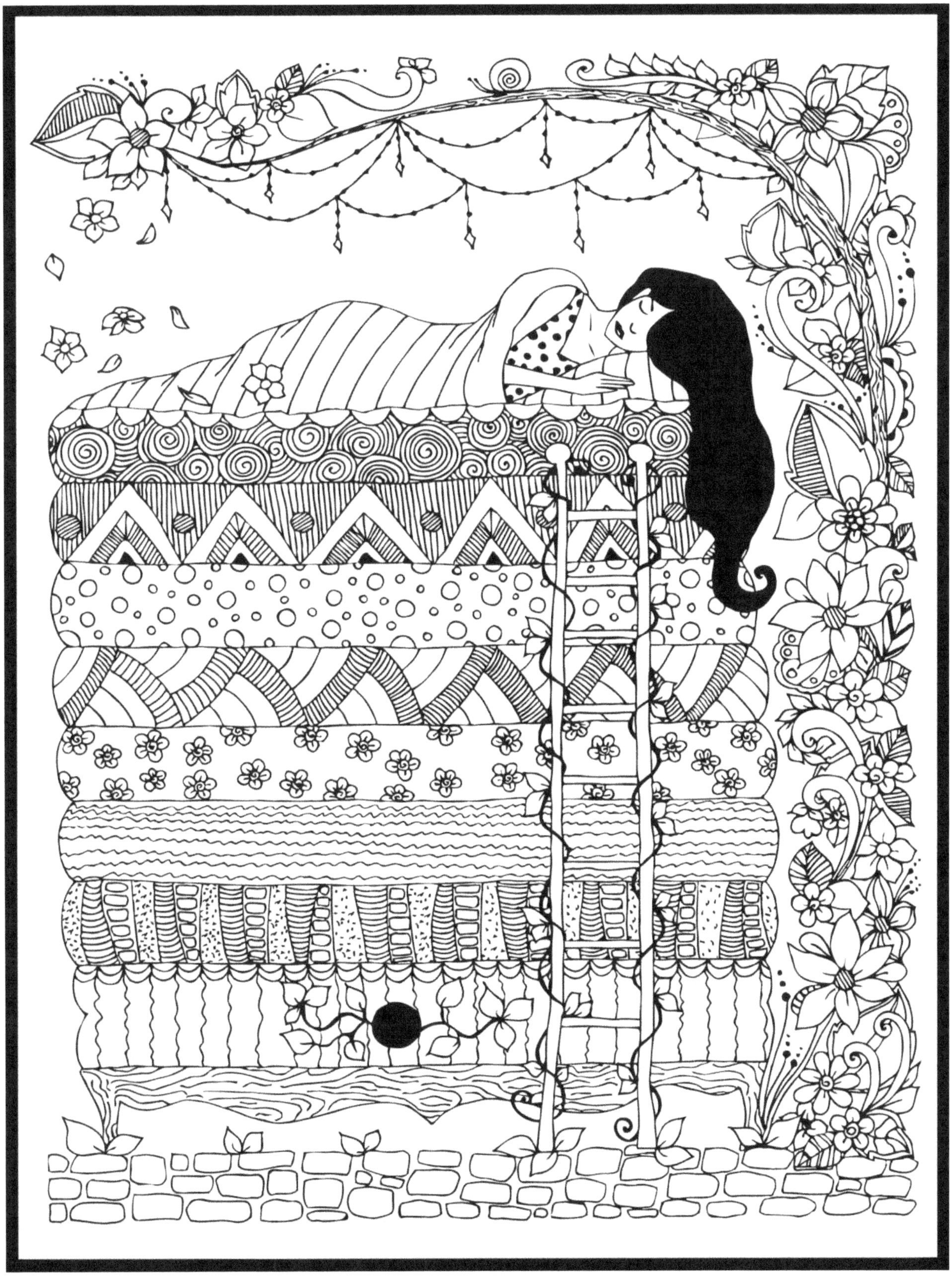

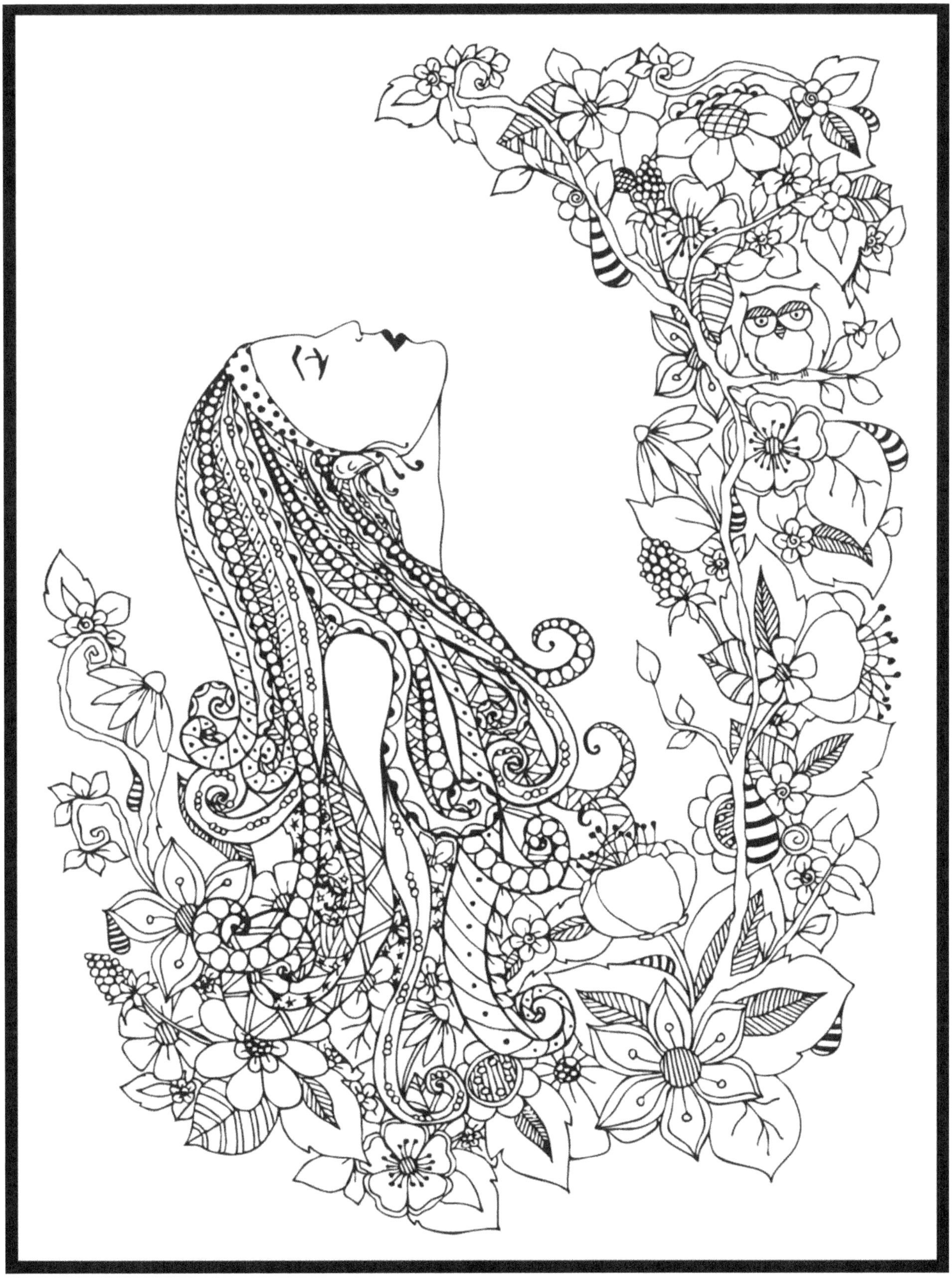

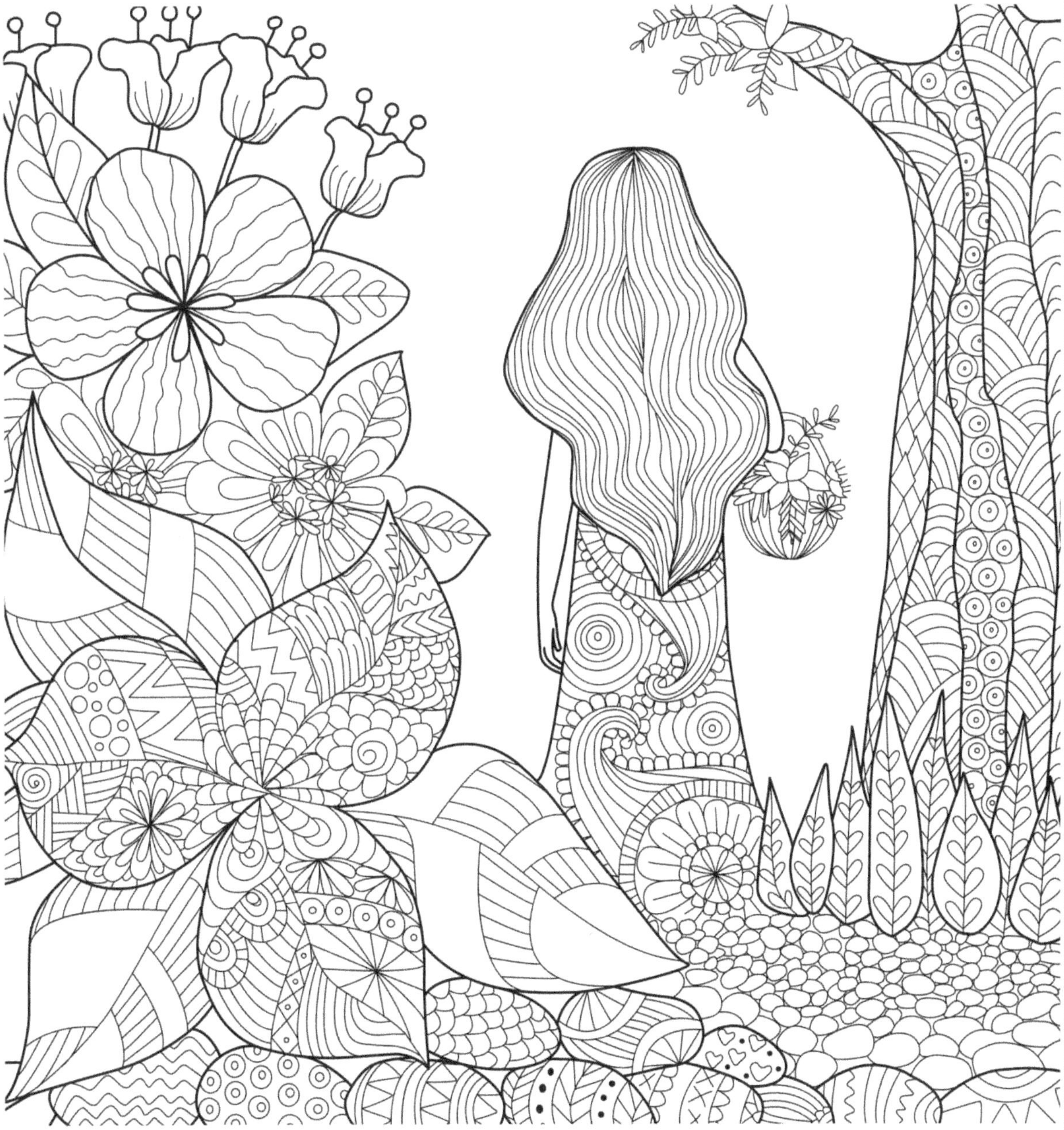

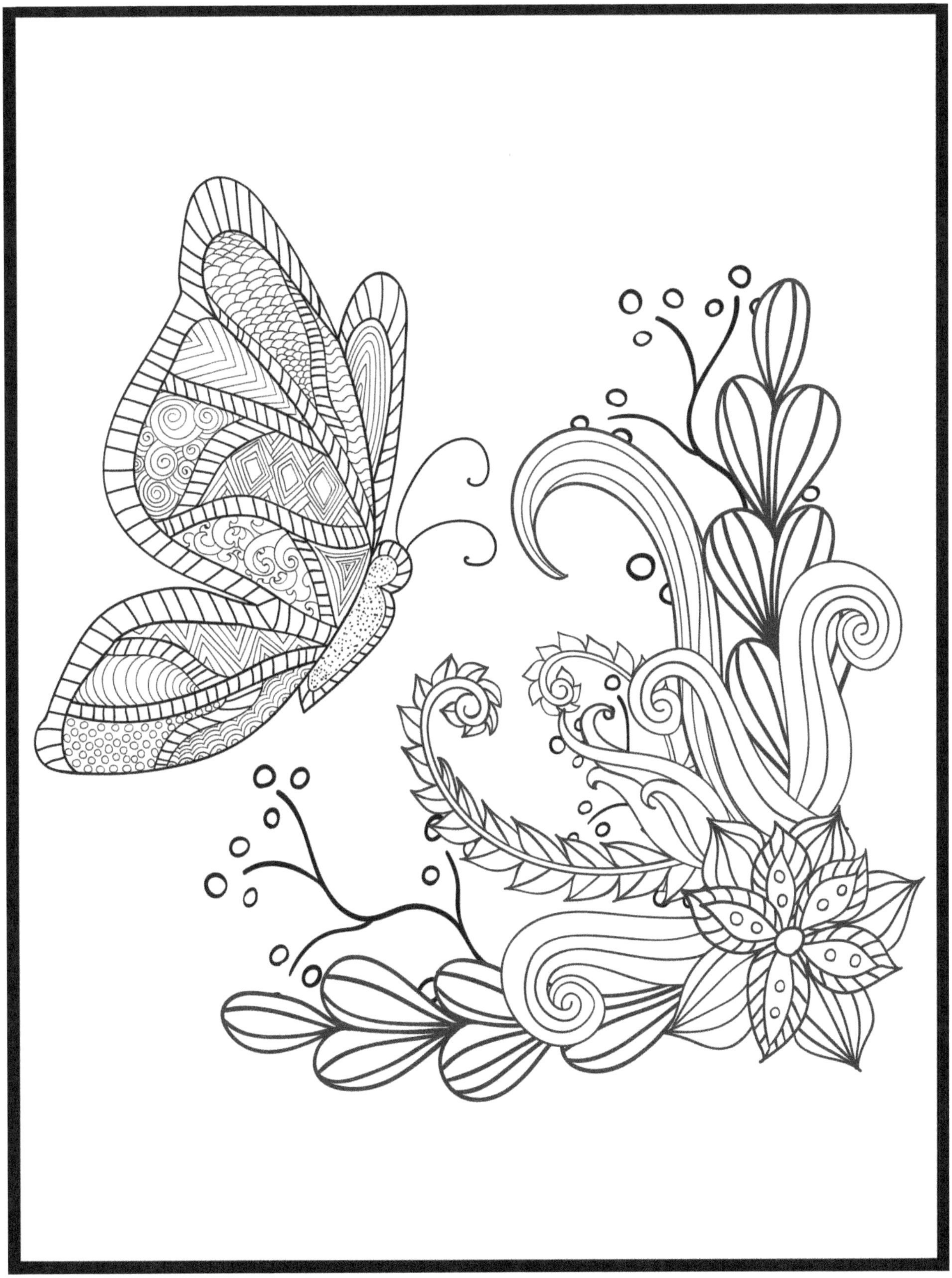

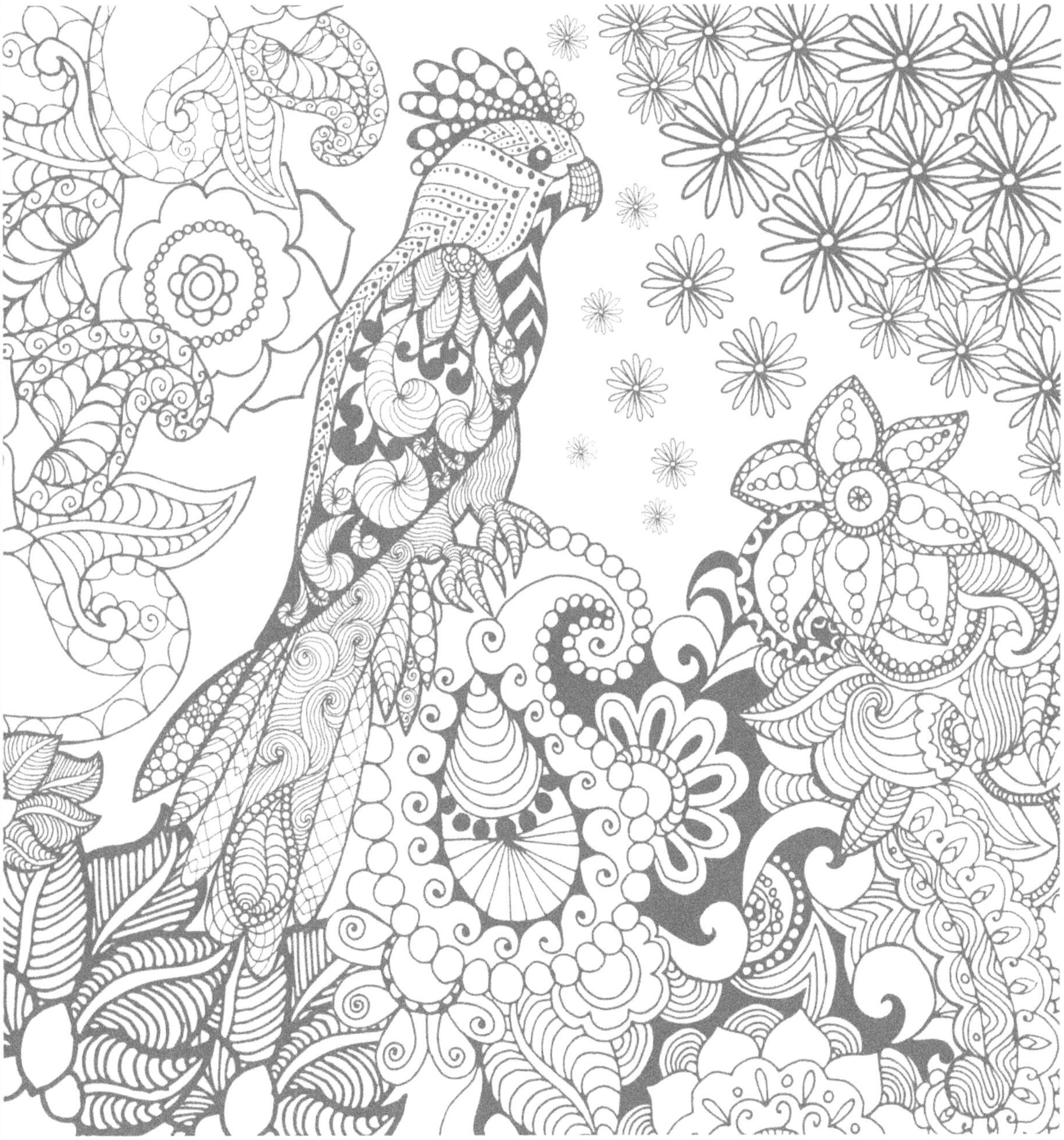

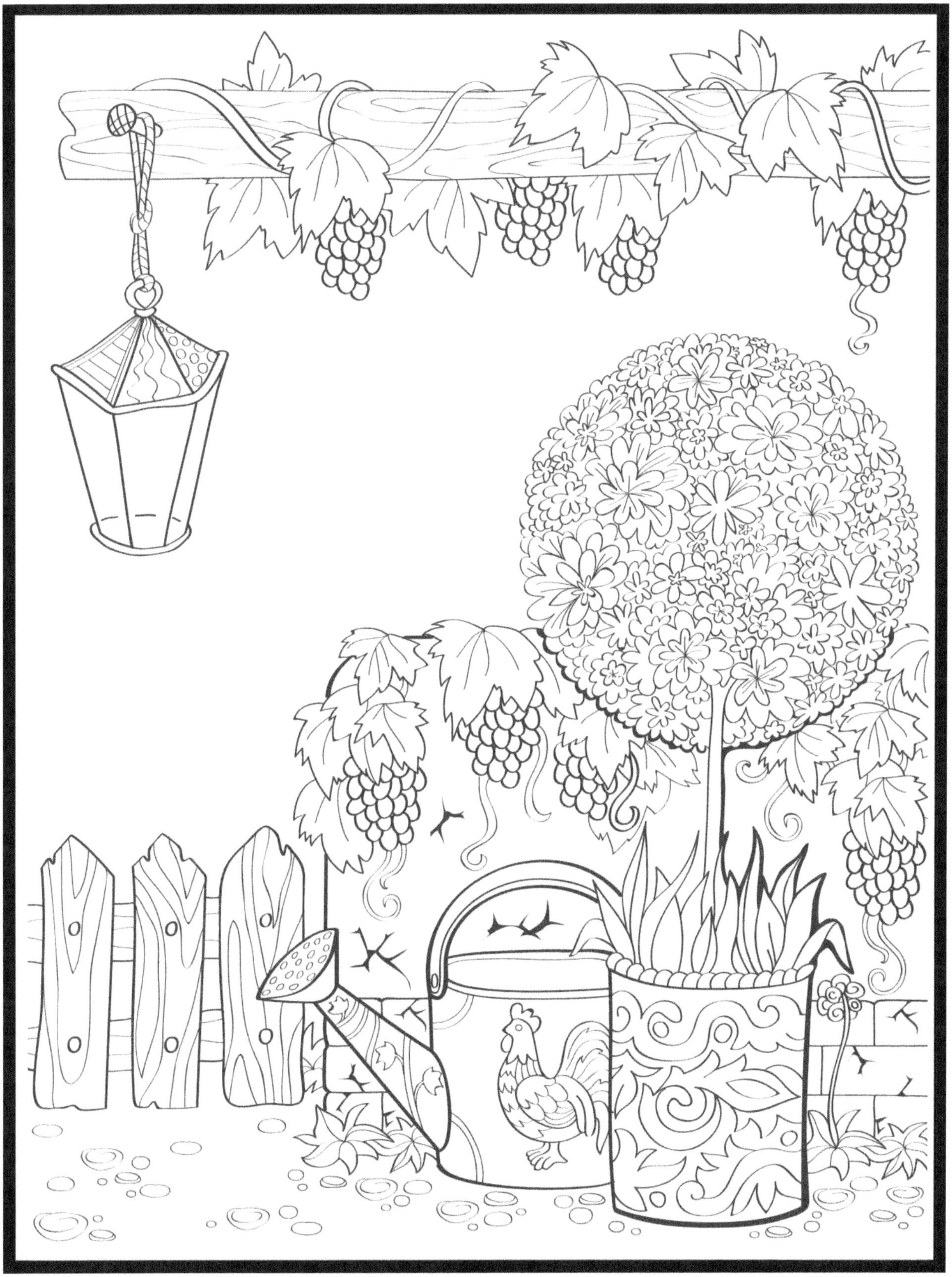

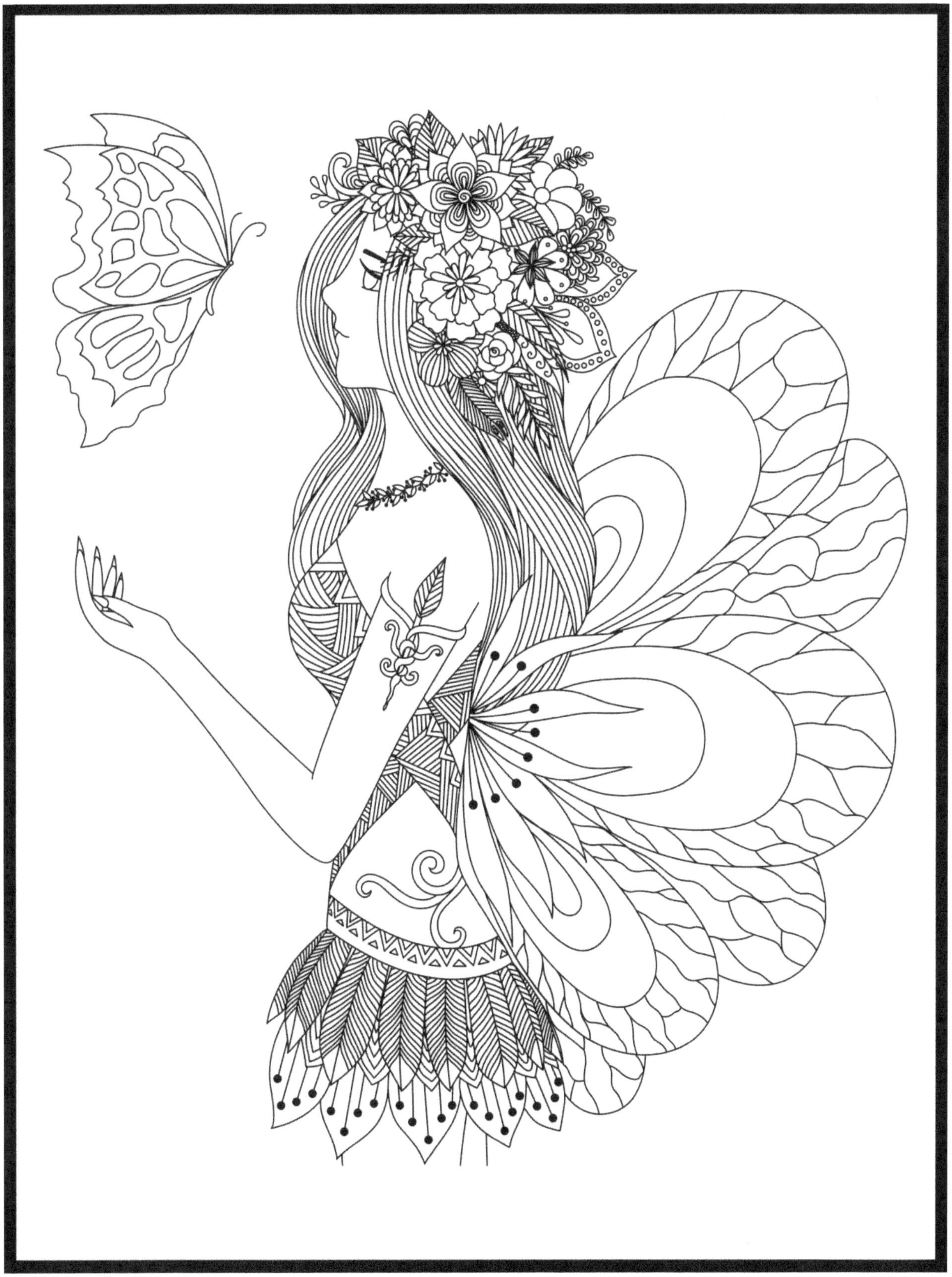

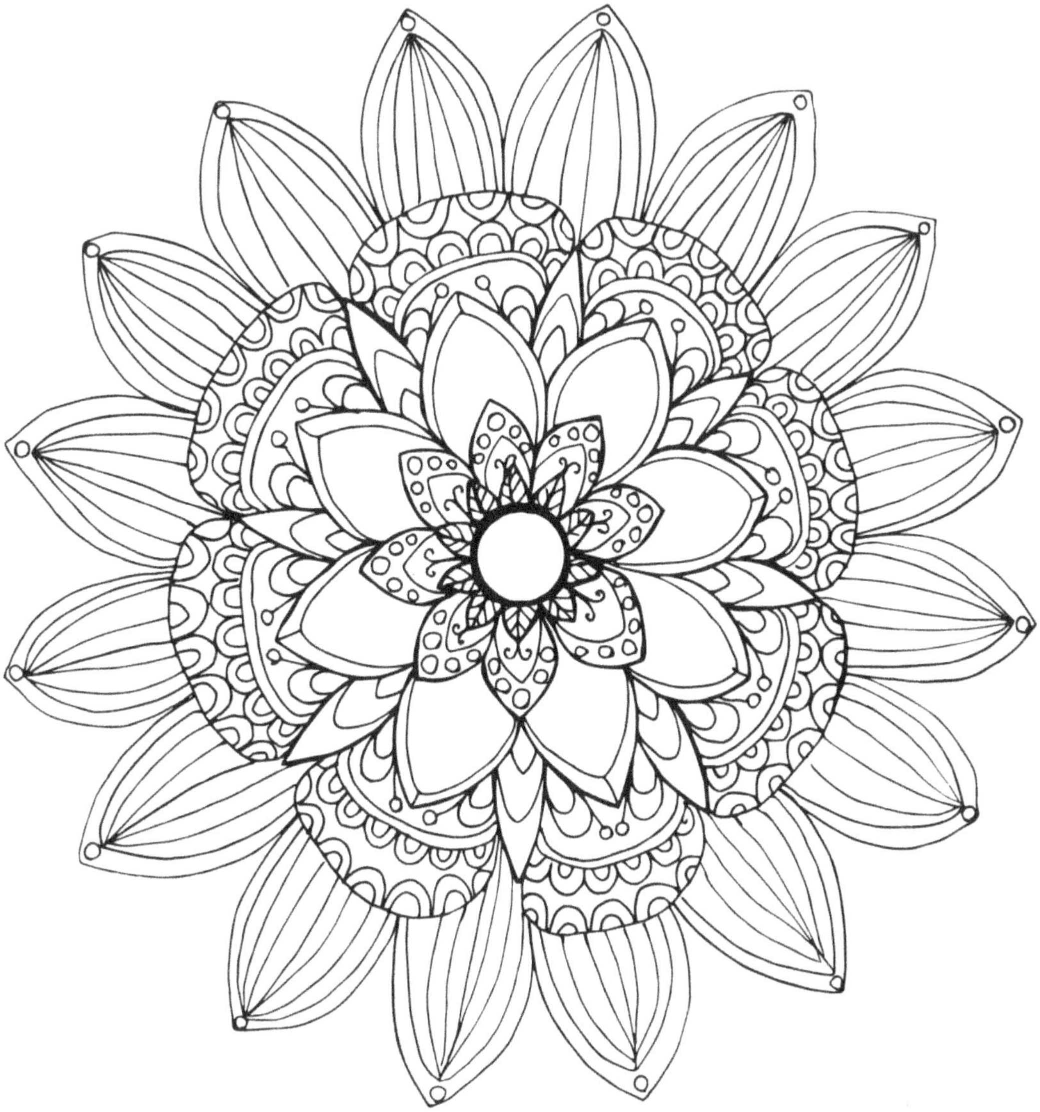

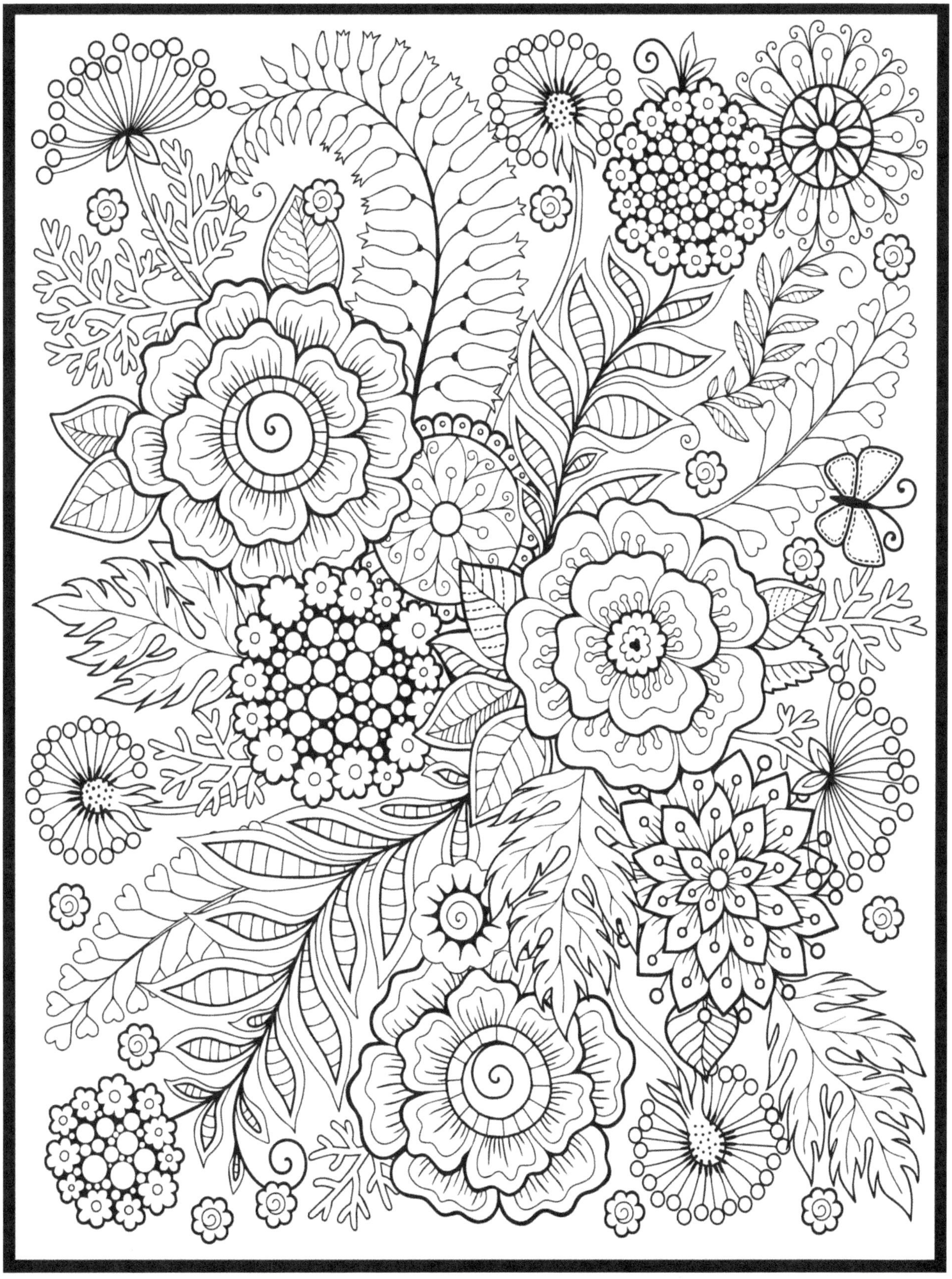

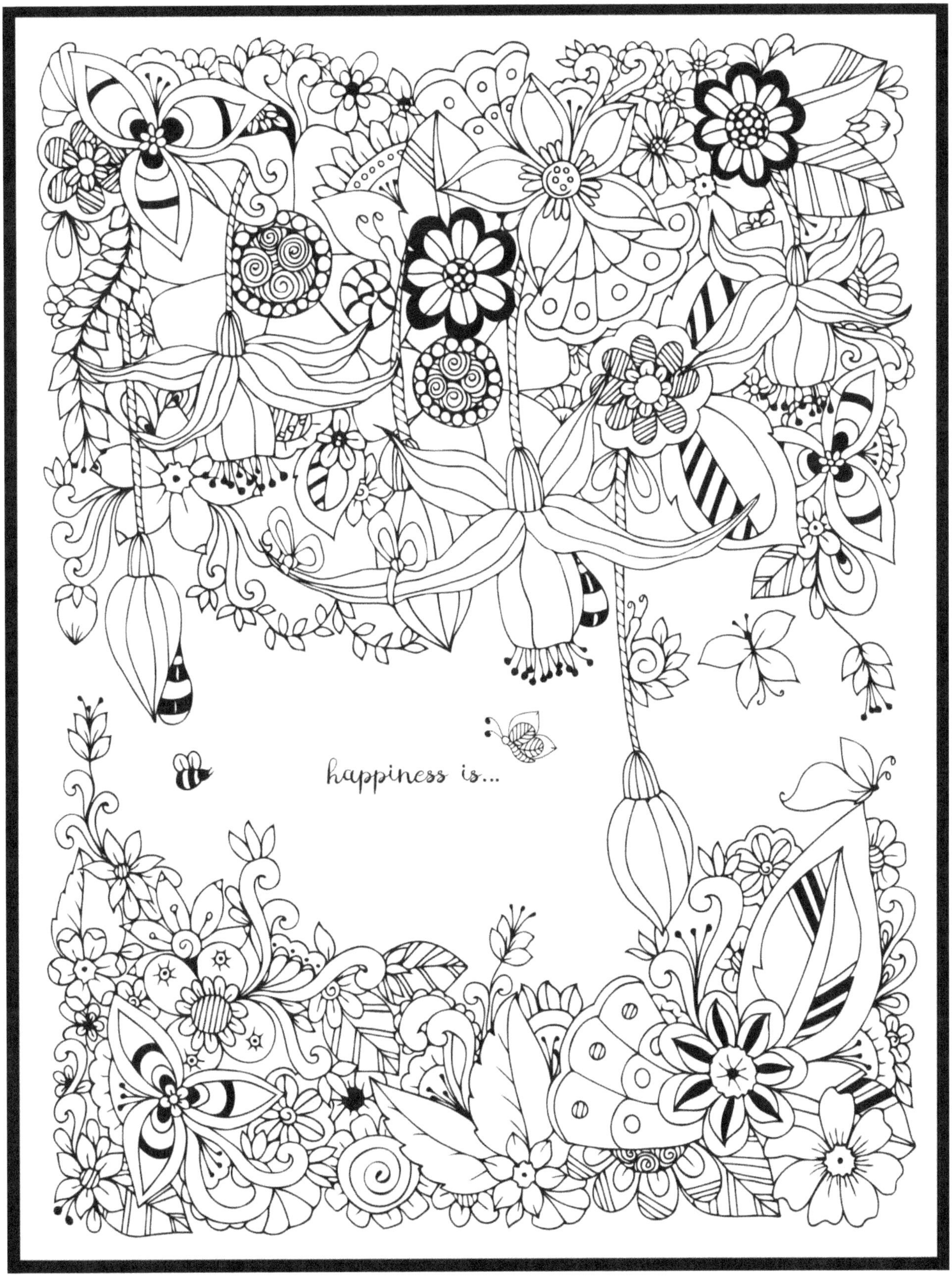
happiness is...

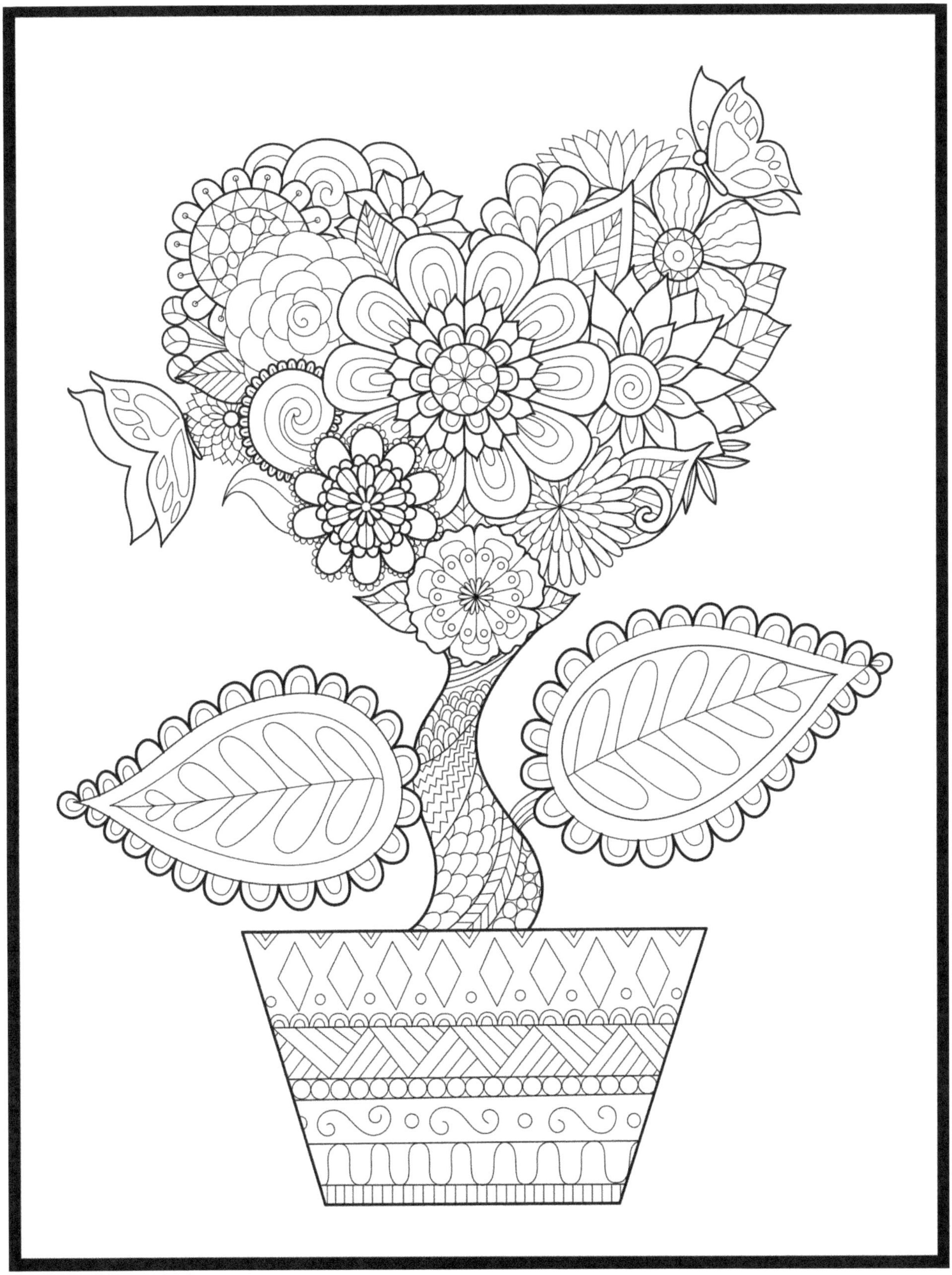

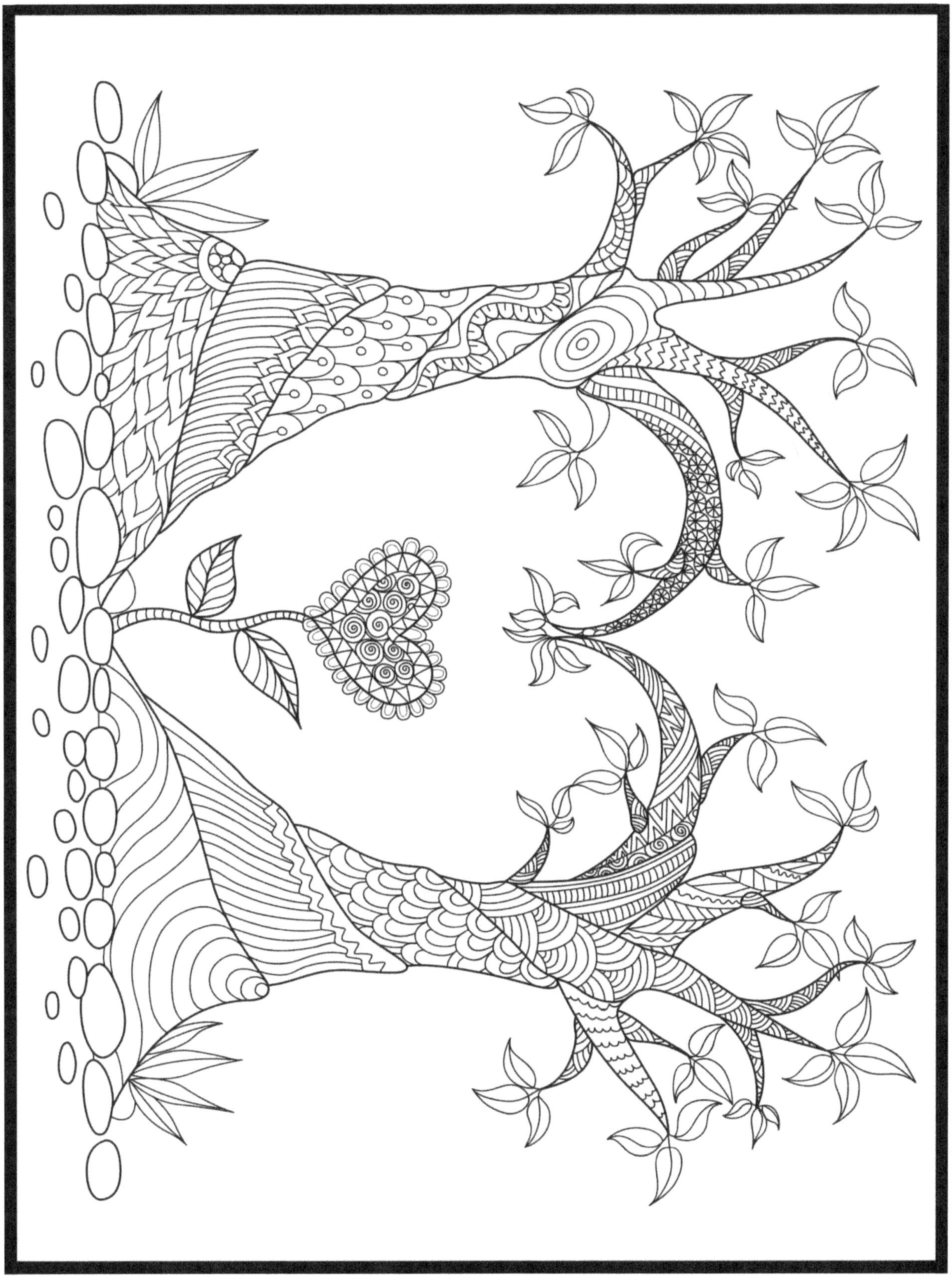

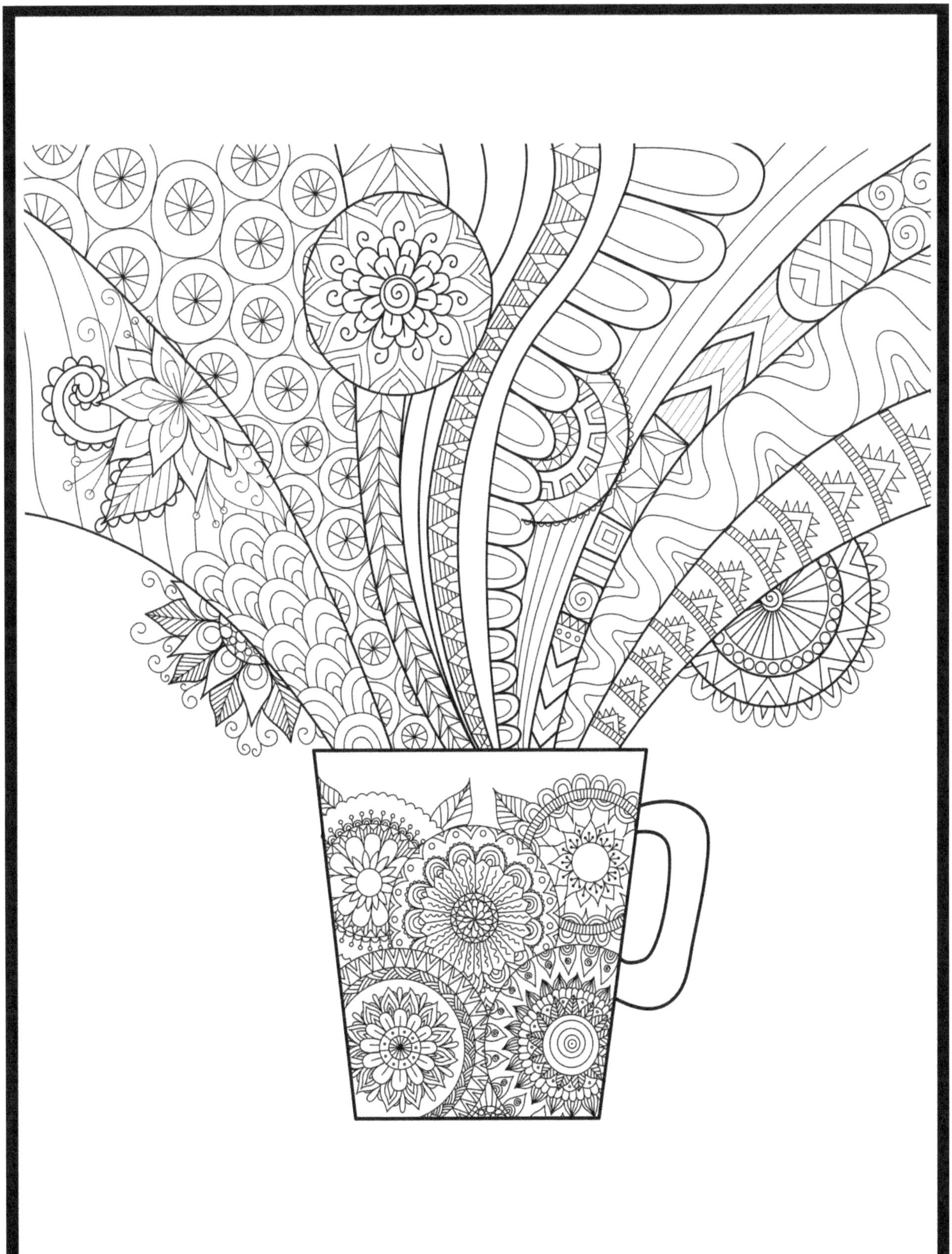

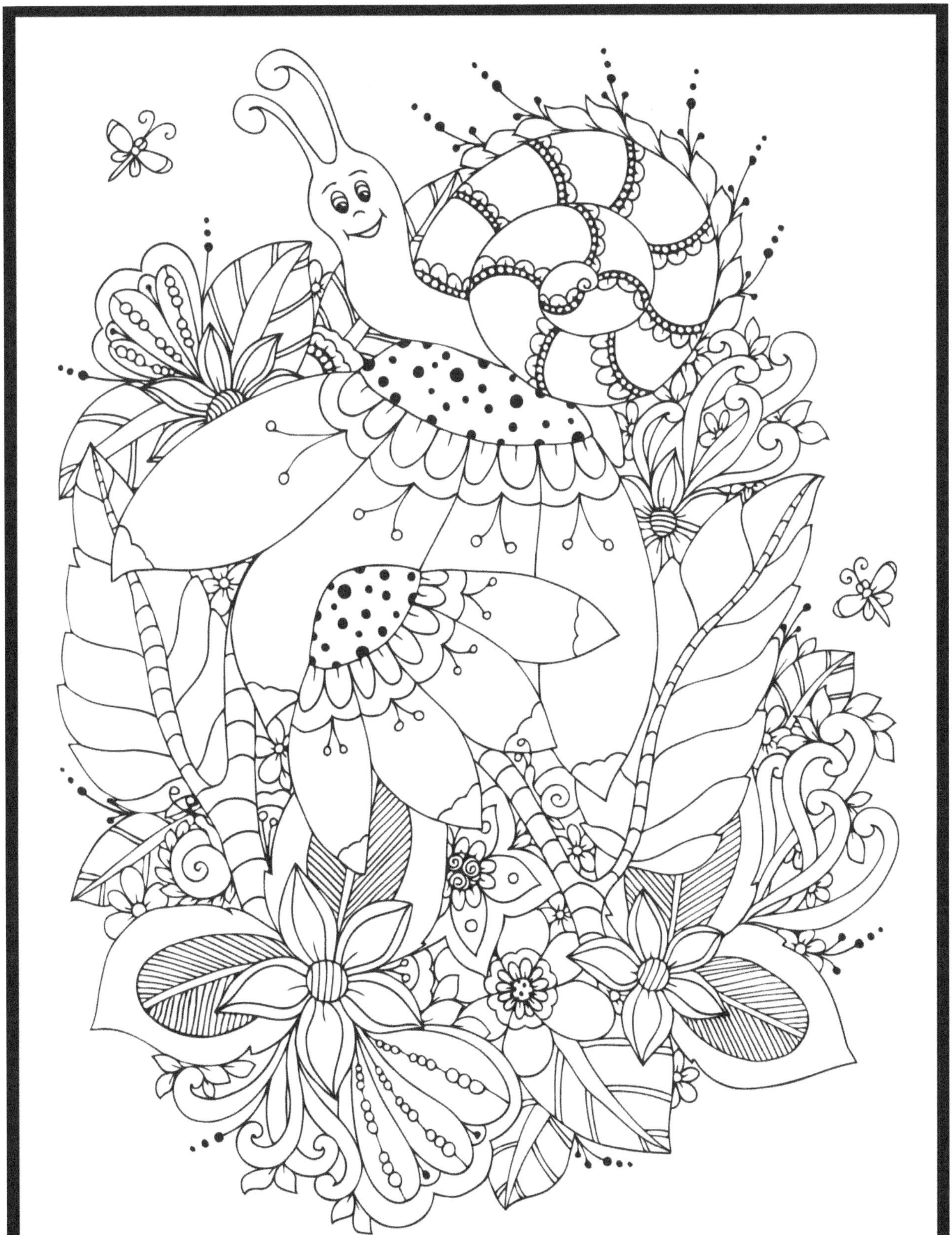

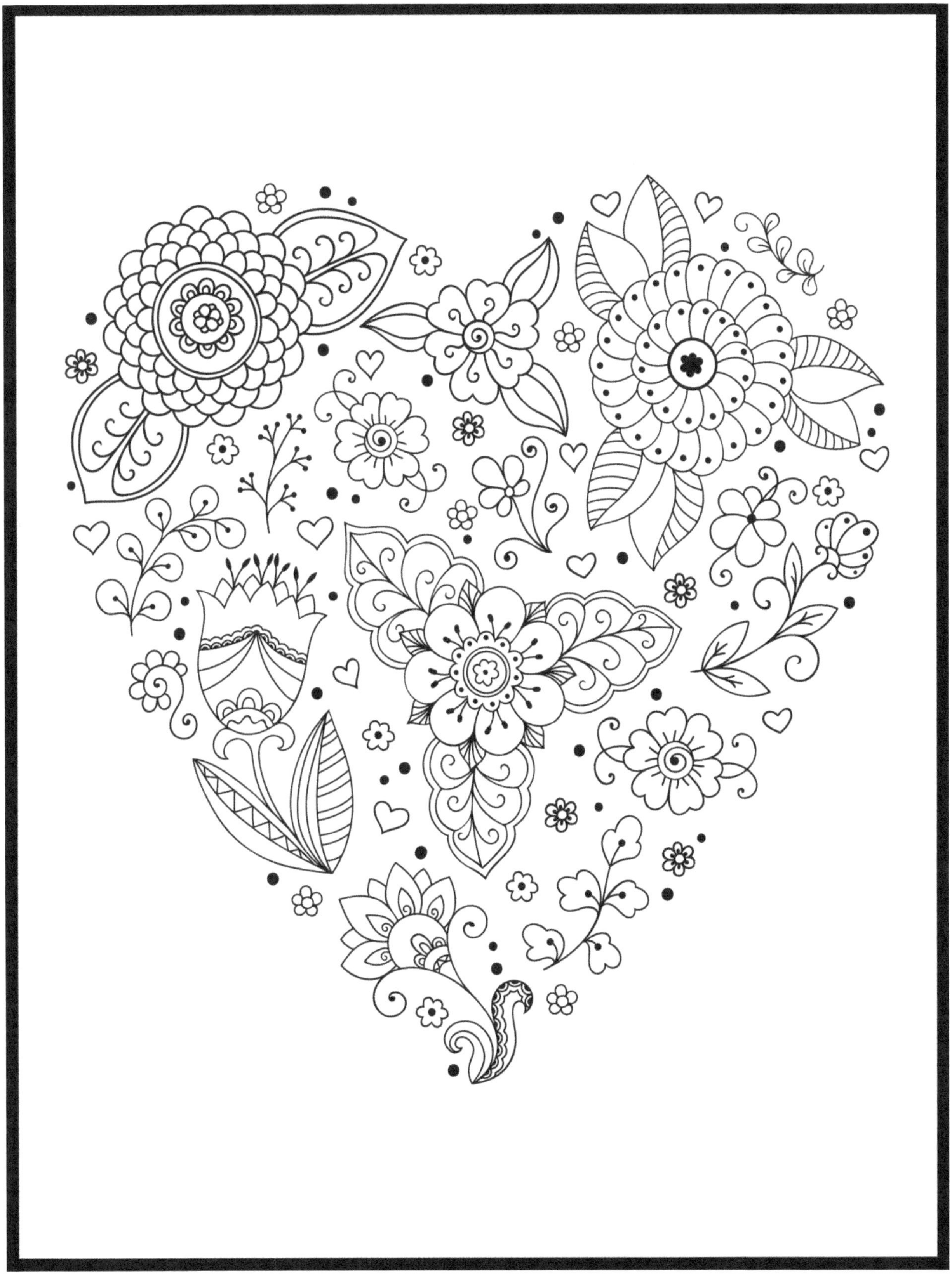

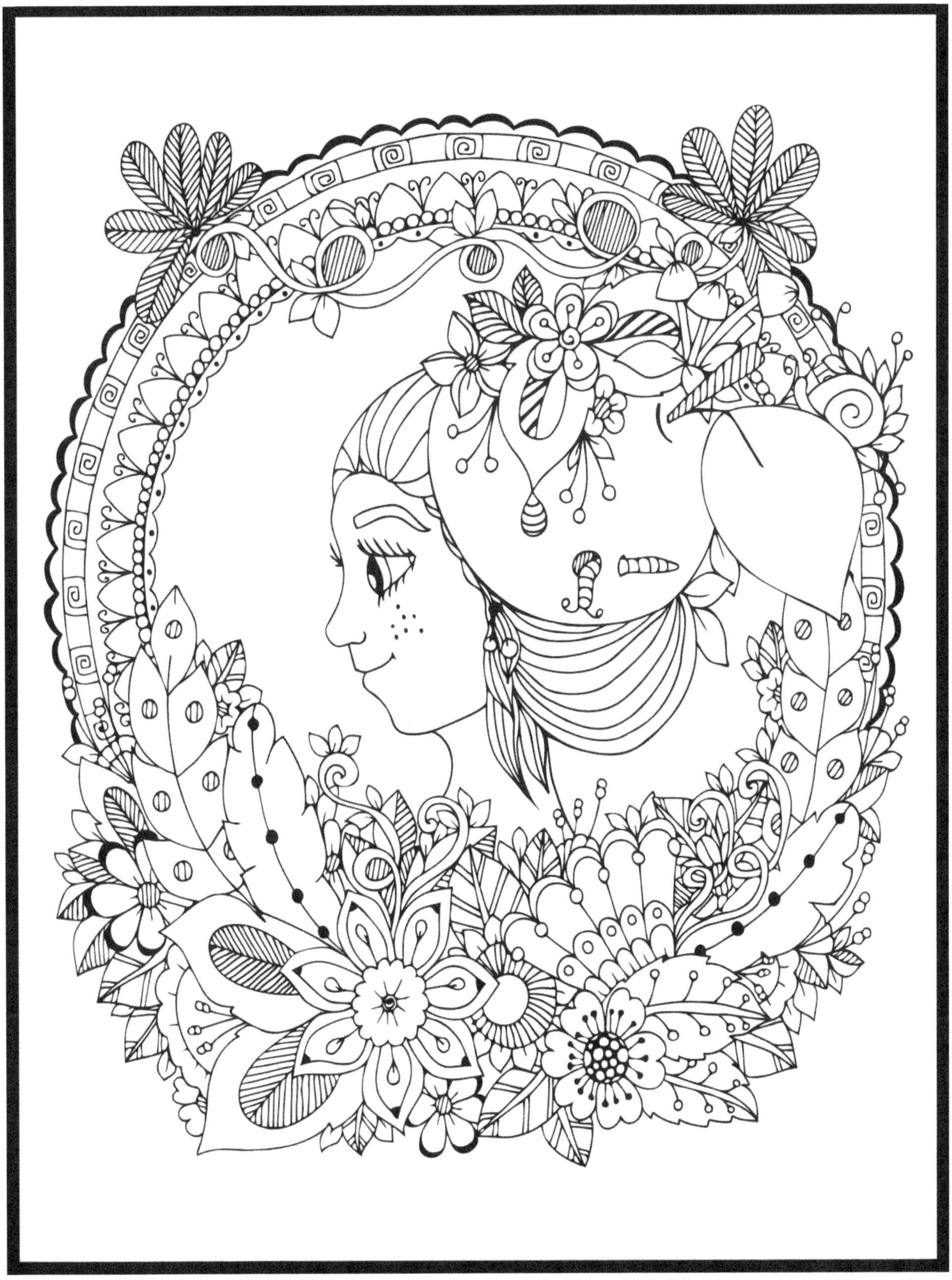

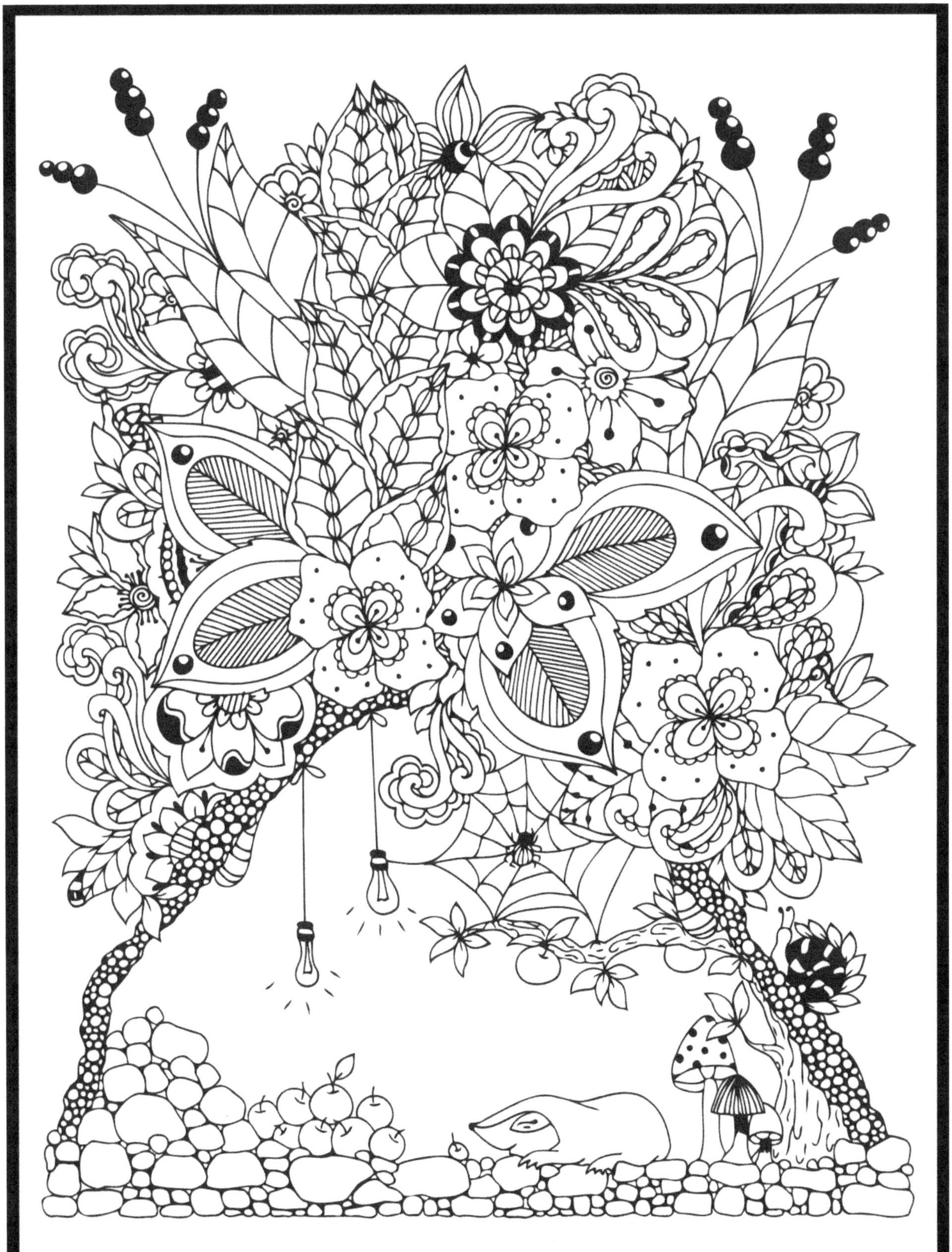

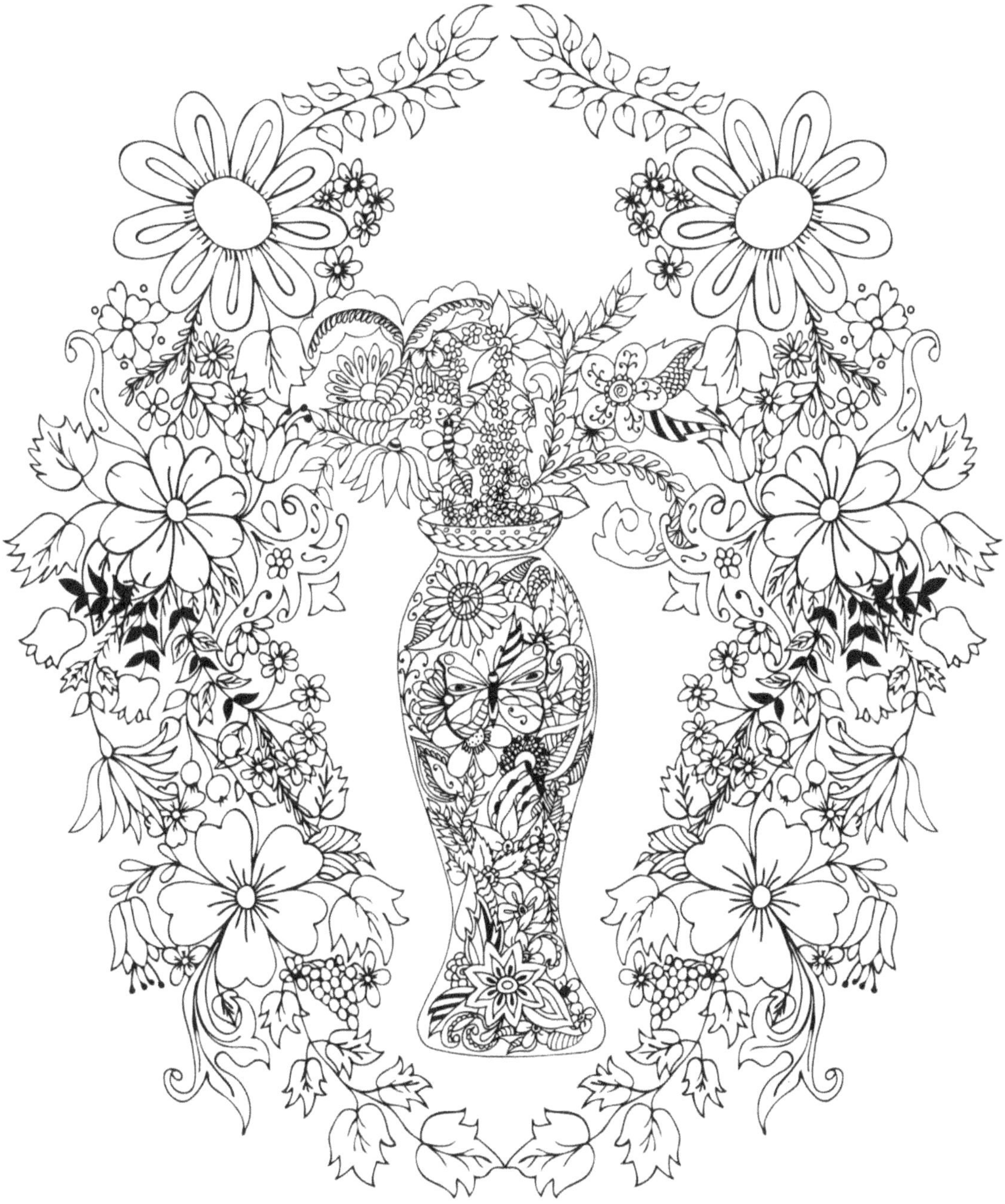

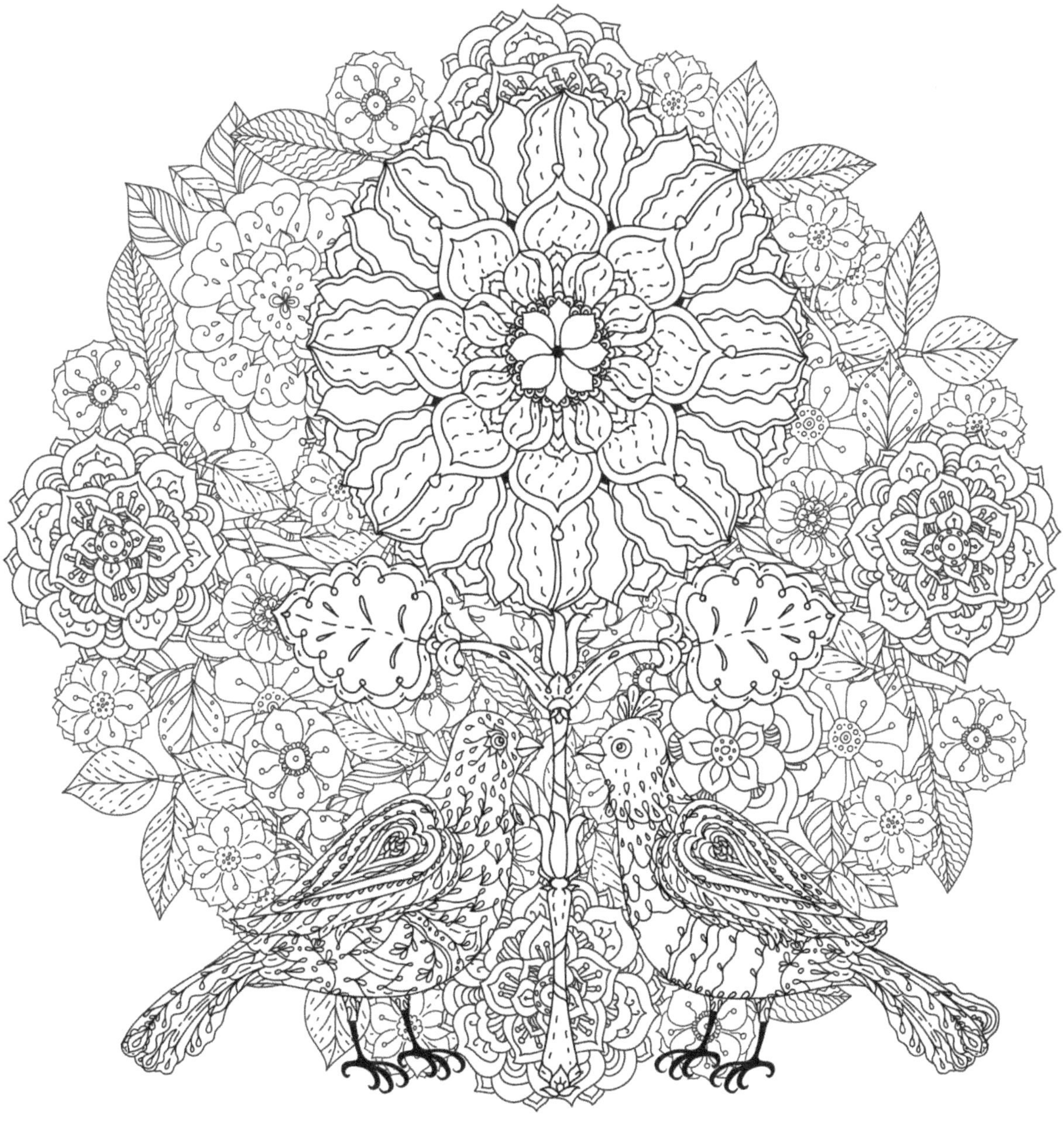

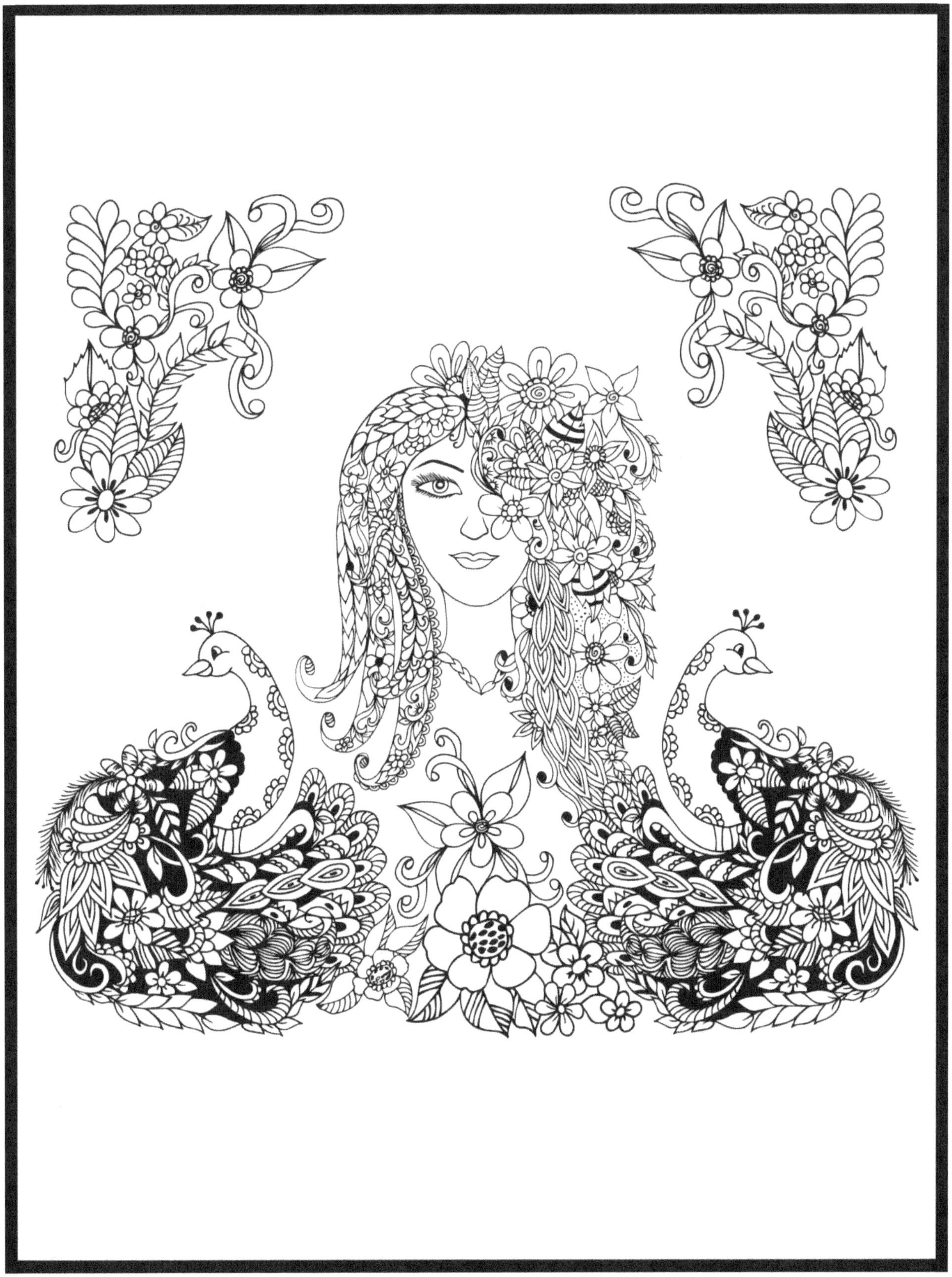

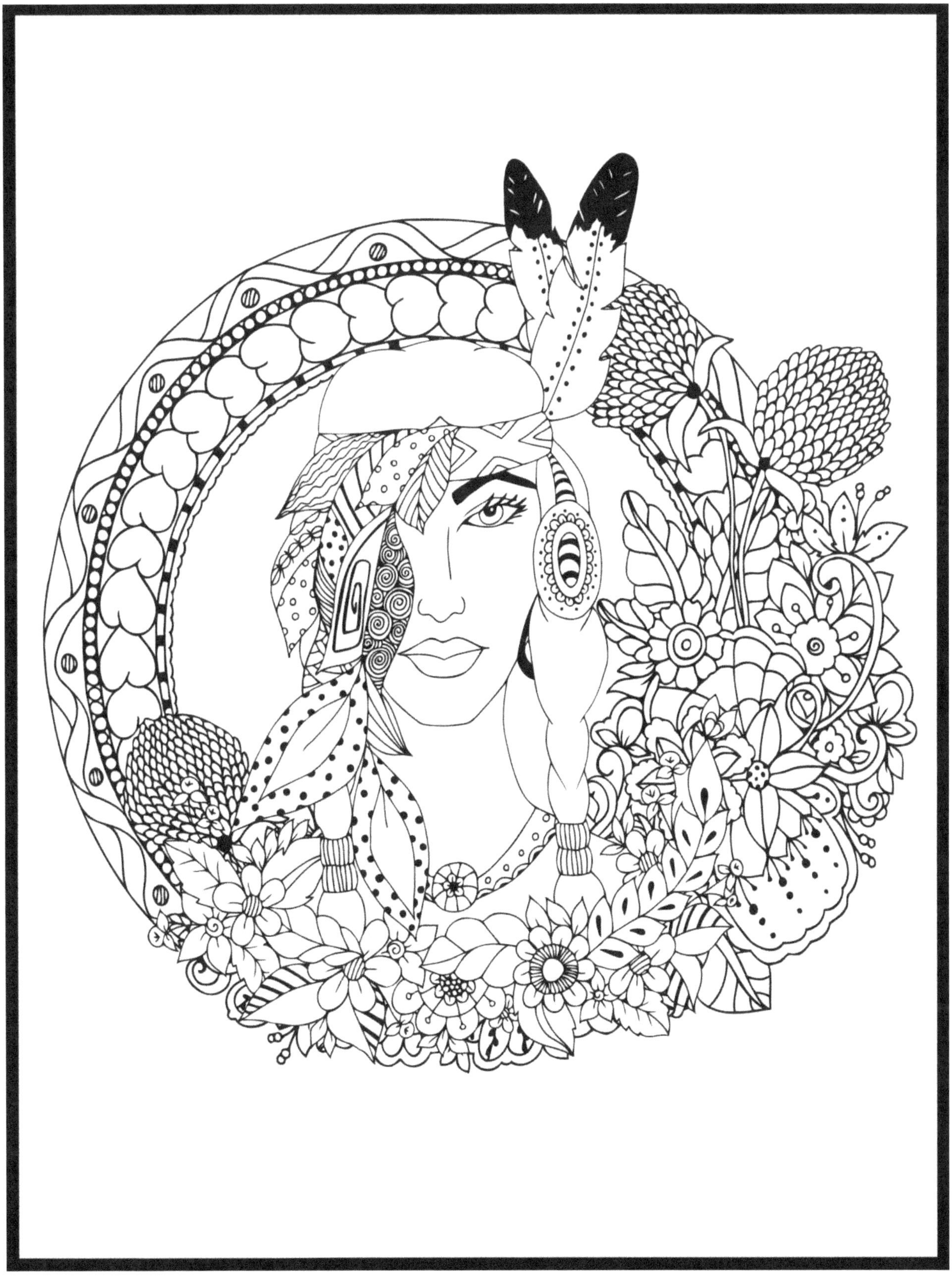

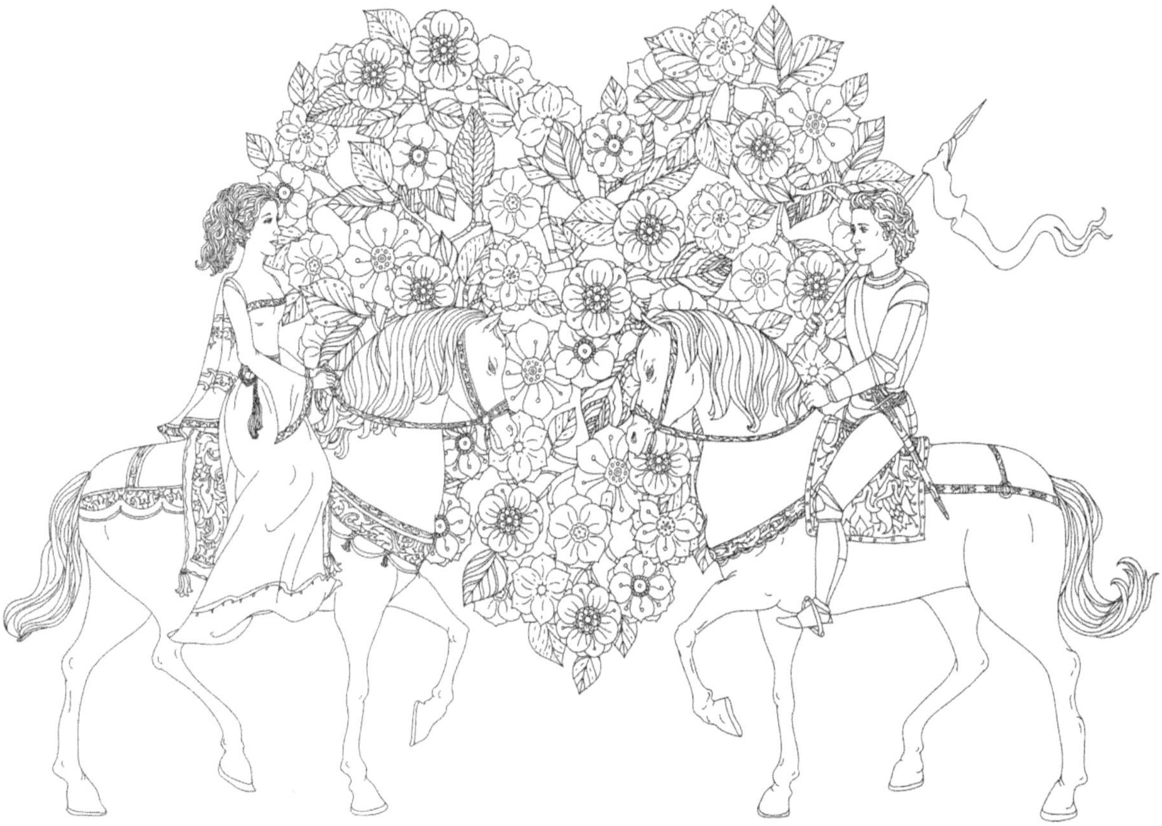

www.ingramcontent.com/pod-product-compliance
Lightning Source LLC
Chambersburg PA
CBHW080742240526
45472CB00025B/2212
* 9 7 8 1 7 1 9 0 6 9 8 8 5 *